D0008072

things you get for free

things you get for free

Michael McGirr

Atlantic Monthly Press
New York

BRIDGEWATER PUBLIC LIBRARY
15 SOUTH STREET
BRIDGEWATER, MA 02324

Every word of this book is true.
Any resemblances of actual persons
to fictional characters
is entirely their own fault.

Every reasonable endeavour has been made to contact relevant copyright holders. Where
this has not proved possible, the copyright holders are invited to contact the publisher.

Copyright © 2000 by Michael McGirr

All rights reserved. No part of this book may be reproduced in any form or by any
electronic or mechanical means, including information storage and retrieval systems,
without permission in writing from the publisher, except by a reviewer, who may quote
brief passages in a review. Any members of educational institutions wishing to
photocopy part or all of the work for classroom use, or publishers who would like to
obtain permission to include the work in an anthology, should send their inquiries to
Grove/Atlantic, Inc., 841 Broadway, New York, NY 10003.

First published in 2000 by Pan Macmillan Australia Pty Limited,
Sydney, Australia

Published simultaneously in Canada
Printed in the United States of America

FIRST AMERICAN EDITION

Library of Congress Cataloging-in-Publication Data

McGirr, Michael, 1961–
    Things you get for free / Michael McGirr.
        p. cm.
    Originally published: Sydney, Australia : Picador, 2000.
    ISBN 0-87113-837-9
    1. McGirr, Michael, 1961—Journeys—Europe. 2. Europe—Description and travel.
3. McGirr, Michael, 1961– 4. Jesuits—Australia—Biography. I. Title.

BX4705.M47617 A3 2002
828'.603—dc21
[B]   2001046418

Design by Greendot Design

Atlantic Monthly Press
841 Broadway
New York, NY 10003

02 03 04 05   10 9 8 7 6 5 4 3 2 1

for mum

5/9/02

Thanks

This book is full of that tyrannical little word, 'I'. But it wouldn't exist without the efforts of 'we'. Mum and I travelled for a little over six weeks. I worked on this account of the trip for a little over three and a half years. It's lucky we came home when we did. There are many people, family, friends and colleagues, to whom I am deeply grateful for comments, suggestions and encouragement: Linda, Joseph, Kerin, Nona, Peter, Tim W, Meg, Bryony, Morag, Kate, Lisa C, Kristen, Wendy, Tim C, Thea, Helen, Amanda L, Rod, David, Jonathan, Loretta, Bill, Lisa J, Maria, Michele, Peter, Genevieve, Nicole and Janet. I am also grateful to Jesuit friends who patiently read drafts: Richard, Dan, Peter H, Peter S, Andrew H, Andrew B, Stephen S. I am grateful to Peter Bishop and the Varuna Writers' Centre at Katoomba for the time and space they offer. I am grateful to Fran Bryson, my agent, Judith Lukin-Amundsen, the book's editor, and Nikki Christer, its Australian publisher. I am grateful to Maria Massie, my U.S. agent, and Morgan Entrekin and Daniel Maurer at Grove/Atlantic, Inc. Above all, I am grateful to Mum for sitting for the portrait.

'Tell the truth but tell it Slant'
– Emily Dickinson

*'Religion is at its best when it states the bleeding
obvious'*
– Margaret Simons

One

I WAS WITH MY MOTHER when she bought her suitcase, but I didn't see her pack. The suitcase took a lot of finding. It had to satisfy a list of criteria. It needed wheels. It needed a compartment for wet clothes. It needed extra room for all the stuff that we'd get for free from hotels and airlines. It had to be strong.

'Not like the case your father got me for our wedding. You remember the one.'

Mum's questions often sound like statements. I couldn't visualise the bag she was talking about.

'He gave me a suitcase but it got mildew in it and fell apart. I had to throw it out.'

Suddenly I remembered. It was a huge yellow thing. If ever it was full, you would have needed six pallbearers to lift it. The very sight of it spoke oceans about Mum and Dad's idea of travel when they married in 1959. They had booked to travel to England on the *Fairstar* and had already been down to look over their cabin before the wedding to work out how they were going to get their luggage into such a confined space. Mum's bag was built to accommodate half a dozen loosely packed frocks and other delicate items. Shoes travelled separately. As did cosmetics. As did hats. As did children, if you had them. The result was a suitcase the size of a life-boat with a single flimsy handle and a couple of half-hearted locks. It was made of cardboard and designed for bulk not weight.

Mum's big trip with Dad never eventuated. The bag spent years slowly rotting under the house in an area which seemed to have been specially hollowed out to make room for it. The day we took it to the tip, after Dad died, the house lurched slightly on an unaccustomed vacuum.

~

My mother, like myself, is a great believer in the Things You Get For Free. She has almost fifty fridge magnets in the kitchen, all of them give-aways from the businesses they advertise. Over thirty of them, in fact, come from the pharmacy where she works. We grew up washing our hair and fighting acne with the free sample sachets she got from pharmaceutical companies. Mum isn't mean. She is dangerously generous. But she was never going to buy a new suitcase when she was always on the verge of winning one on the wheel at a local fete and the fete needed her support. Over the years, she has bought enough tickets to kit the Australian army.

Mum spent years planning her first trip overseas. She never bought a guidebook. Her preference was always for what she calls 'literature'. 'Literature' refers to the glossy brochures you get for free from travel agents. Mum was a junkie for them. She'd often drop by and pick a few up when she was feeling low.

'Have you got any literature on England?' she'd ask.

No agent ever misunderstood what she meant. When we were little, Mum would prop herself up in bed, get one of us to massage her feet, and read the fine print about package holidays until Dad decided he wanted to go to bed and threw us out of their bedroom. One result of Mum's fantasy life was that our school geography projects, however ignorant, were always the best illustrated in the class. The other was that Mum became exceptionally well informed about a certain type of travel.

In 1996, when I was thirty-four and had been a Jesuit priest for a couple of years, I managed to organise about six weeks off work. I suggested to Mum that we do the trip she and Dad had planned so long before. Mum swung into action. She booked flights to and from England, with a free side flight to Rome. She booked two weeks' car hire with bed-and-breakfast vouchers in Britain. She booked a ten-day package tour of Italy. She booked trains for us to go to Paris.

'You've obviously done this before,' said Craig, the travel agent.

'First time overseas for me and first time out of Asia for my son,' said Mum. She was the star rookie. She discovered that if you booked a second tour with the group that was taking us to Italy, you got a discount. So we booked to do Belgium, Germany, Switzerland and Paris in seven days. They weren't to belong precisely to the category of things she got for free, but we were to be the first travellers in history who went to those places to save money.

'Is that it?' asked Craig. He seemed a little disappointed that we were sticking to such a tried and true itinerary.

'We've boldly vowed to go where millions have gone before,' I announced.

'I must tell you one thing.' Craig looked serious.

'What's that?' Mum was turning to the back of a brochure where she could show him that whatever he had to say she had already read the fine print about it.

'I must tell you that you are going at the busiest time of year. These places will be pretty hot. And crowded,' I added.

'The crowds in the European summer can be incredible.'

'It doesn't matter,' said Mum. 'I want to arrive in Rome on the Feast of Our Lady of Perpetual Succour.'

This obviously didn't mean much to Craig.

'I want to be there on June 27. My wedding anniversary.'

We got free vinyl cabin bags from the company with which we'd booked our bus tours. Even so, Mum still wanted to buy a bag with wheels. And, as it turned out, she wanted one with a few secret pockets where she could keep stuff hidden. Stuff she wanted with her on the other side of the world, in the place her father had come from.

When I think of my father, he is getting into a car. He is getting out of the house. He has his Gladstone bag. He needs to get out, to go some-where. He doesn't know where.

Two

I HAVE A THING WITH BAGS. When I was twenty, I moved from Sydney to Melbourne to live in a house which had an enormous number of suitcases in the cellar. I had been nearing the end of my final year of high school when Dad died and I joined the Jesuit novitiate in a bit of a rush the following February. I didn't cope with Dad's illness well, and I coped with his death even worse, so I ran away. At least, that is what I thought for years. I didn't realise at the time that my decision, impulsive as it was, was more complex than mere flight. I was desperate to get out of home. But buried deep inside that desperation was a need to lose something so I'd know how much I valued it, a need to feel homesick. I also had a buried talent to give and receive love. For free. It was years before I could recognise this. By then it was well and truly time to go on a trip with my mother.

Our noviceship had been a gruelling experience. Far from helping me come to terms with myself so that at the end of two years I could freely commit to a life of poverty, chastity and obedience in the Jesuit order, it pushed important issues under the surface until they nearly drowned. Especially those famous first cousins, grief and sex. The main thing I learnt was how to survive on my own. I spent a lot of time in a musty music room that had been improvised under the novitiate. The walls were lined with old egg cartons and painted bright orange. We had a turntable, a patchy collection of vinyl records and some cumbersome headphones which felt like industrial noise-protectors. They were as close-fitting and almost as heavy as a helmet. I felt safe inside them and used them late at night to listen over and over to the same few records: Supertramp, Fleetwood Mac, Dire Straits. At the same time, I painstakingly sharpened my wit and built a wall around myself with humour. It was a wall covered in soft green ivy and most of the people in the community loved it. But it was still a wall.

~

At the end of the novitiate I moved to our house of studies in Melbourne, a mansion on top of Studley Park Hill which had been built at the end of the previous century by one of the city's leading merchants. In its day, it enabled him to look over his warehouses on the industrial flats below in Collingwood, the other side of the Yarra River. By the time I got there, the Jesuits were using it as a retreat house, a retirement home for elderly priests and brothers and a place for students for the priesthood, such as myself, to live. We had a great life. We played cricket on summer evenings while the old priests looked on and wished they were young again. We tossed a frisbee after lunch through the branches of the ancient oak tree which dominated the front lawn. We watched the oak change with the seasons. I guessed I was happy.

In fact, I was emotionally comatose. I had lots of company but few friends. My head was completely divorced from the rest of my body. It floated on top of my shoulders in a kind of miasma, feeding itself on books and banter. It didn't really care what happened to the rest of me.

I started eating when I wasn't hungry. I began drinking large quantities of cheap cask wine. Riding to class on a bicycle every day down Studley Park Hill, I started to let go of the handlebars, even when heavy traffic was whistling past. I was tempting fate. I would have been half relieved to have been knocked off.

My depression was like God. It was invisible. Its power was subtle, its existence more comfortable to deny. Only once did it manifest itself to me openly.

I was under the house one day looking for parts to repair my bike, when I had a close look for the first time at the pile of suitcases there. There must have been forty or fifty of them. Some quite old. Many of them had tags on them. I recognised the names of a few dead or elderly Jesuits: one had been the head of a big school, another a respected psychologist. One, Noel, had recently retired as a prominent thinker and theologian. I thought that each of these men moved from house to house with their entire world in the bag that carried their name. I was wrong about that, of course. They may have shifted their belongings in one bag but not their worlds. Their worlds shifted them.

Inside many of the bags were still more bags. Somebody had obviously put smaller ones inside big

ones to save a bit of room. Eventually, I came across a
bag which had once belonged to an older man who was
still living in the house. He was a man whom I came to
love deeply. This man was famous for having had a
tough time in the order. He had tried to teach school
but the kids toyed with his gentle, even effeminate,
manner; he had gone to England to take up a long-
nurtured vocation as a Benedictine monk but that dream
fell apart. He returned to Australia with his confidence
in shreds and became silent and withdrawn. Eventually
he resurfaced into soft-hued twilight years, but the
return journey involved enormous personal risks. On
the way, he had spent years barely able to cross the road
on his own. When he showered he went into the cubicle in his complete old-fashioned clerical kit and
emerged dressed exactly the same way, terrified that
somebody might see his body. His suitcase, sitting in the
jaws of a bigger one, was plastered with baggage checks
for England: it was tattooed with reminders of his failure. Inside were two threadbare shirts. There was also
a yellowing copy of a newspaper from 1961, carrying
an obituary of his father.

For some reason, when I opened the bag, I got a
lump in my throat. I sat in a broken desk chair which
was also under the house and watched one solitary tear
land on the grime on top of another piece of furniture.
It hardly disturbed the settled pattern of dust. I looked
at it like it belonged to somebody else, as if the old
plumbing must have begun to leak. But it was mine. It
had come from inside my head. Something was beginning to thaw.

Inside my friend's suitcase was a small Globite school

bag. The type that little boys used to pack with lunch on their first day of school. I dusted it and took it back to my room. My heart was stirring from its long hibernation. I told nobody.

~

Later that year I packed a few things into the Globite bag and went away to live for a time in a community of intellectually disabled people on the south coast of New South Wales. The house was part of a network of such communities called 'L'Arche'. L'Arche had then, and still has, a deep understanding of what draws people together and what holds them apart. They are held apart by their inability to be weak or vulnerable with each other and this, in turn, comes from their terror in the face of their own hurt. The intellectually disabled members of a L'Arche are its teachers because their hurt or woundedness tends to be undisguised. That's the theory. I had it down pat from books before I even got to L'Arche. But the reality takes a long time to seep in. Just because you know the lyrics it doesn't mean you can sing the song.

One member of the community had spent years in an enormous institution in Goulburn. At times she was an outrageous, but often delightful, attention seeker. She'd grown up knowing that she had to scream for tenderness. Sometimes she would go to her room, put on a big set of headphones, and listen to the same few records over and over. Somebody who knew her well said that this was her way of grieving. Her favourite was Cliff Richard's 'Wired For Sound'. I didn't share her taste in music. But I suspected, to my alarm, that I shared much else.

In the L'Arche community I fell in love with another of the volunteer helpers. When I returned to Melbourne, on the day of the Ash Wednesday fires in 1983, I told my Jesuit superior that perhaps I should be thinking of a different way of life as I had decided that celibacy was not for me. I planned to return and work for my board in the L'Arche community.

My superior's name was Brendan. He knew more than his prayers. He sent me away for a week to rest and think things over in a small community of Jesuits not far away. This community was notorious among Jesuits for its bad atmosphere. The people in it baited each other all the time. They had developed petty ways to assert themselves and make each other feel small. Brendan always denies it, but I suspect he had a ruse. On the one hand, he was making it as easy as possible for me to leave the order by putting me among such crusty old relics. On the other hand, he was saying that if I chose to remain, these people were as much part of who we were as anybody else. If I wanted to be a Jesuit, I had to take the good with the bad and there was no shortage of bad.

While I was there, a penny dropped. We had prayer at the dinner table every night. It was pretty quick so the gents could go and watch the news on TV and complain bitterly about the communists running the ABC. Three nights in a row we had the same psalm. I thought at first that this was a form of laziness. But they liked the psalm. These guys were like Kerry playing Cliff Richard over and over. They just didn't know how to get out of the groove in which they were stuck. Jesuits tend to have lots of degrees and plenty of success and a reputation for doing things with a certain panache. But under all those cosmetic achievements, a typical Jesuit community is a bit like a L'Arche community.

I have lived with many destitute men. Many Jesuits have been hurt, have caused hurt and live out of fear that any of this might surface. The chassis looks good but the bodywork is full of rust.

I love what's under the duco. That's a big part of why I stuck around. Later that year, the woman I had fallen in love with at L'Arche announced her engagement to somebody else.

~

As they say on TV, there's more. Much more. Ignatius of Loyola, the Basque who started the Jesuits in the sixteenth century, called himself 'The Pilgrim'. His idea of a pilgrimage was not like a packaged tour to Lourdes or Mejugorge, where you have the itinerary before you go and you know exactly what type of spiritual experience you are going to have in advance. Religious tourists get the spiritual experience they pay for. I can't believe that God wants to be controlled quite so much. God doesn't stick to itineraries. I can imagine God slipping quietly away from one of those groups in an airport transit lounge, to join a group of backpackers worried if they can afford a taxi fare. None of the paid-up pilgrims would notice because they have too many photos to take and too much stuff to buy.

Ignatius saw himself on an open-ended journey. For an obsessive character such as he was, this was a perilous way to live. On occasions he did manage to do psychic violence to himself, but came to the happy conclusion that God loves teasing control freaks. If Ignatius

applied to join the Jesuits these days, his interviewers
would draw attention to his tendency to see the spiritual
life as a process of negotiating between extremes, as well
as to his long history of depression, which at least once
brought him to the brink of suicide. Depression was his
companion on some mighty long journeys. So was happiness. But you get the impression he was always caught
unawares by happiness whereas he expected the hard
slog. His leg had been broken in battle. When it set
crookedly, he had it rebroken and set again. He put this
down to vanity. Later, as he dragged himself from one
end of Europe to the other, his limp reminded him of his
days as a soldier when his favourite view had been the
one in the mirror.

One of Ignatius' ideas was that young Jesuits should
undertake a pilgrimage in which they travelled without
money, food or any creature comforts and begged for
anything they needed to survive. His point was not to
discover how resourceful or enterprising a potential
Jesuit could be, but to see how grateful he could become.
Ignatius wasn't interested in how much somebody could
do but how little: the pilgrimage was an invitation to
experience openness, wonder and dependence on the
strange ways in which God provides. It wasn't an
endurance test, although the roads of Reformation
Europe were by no means friendly. Ignatius knew about
mean streets long before Raymond Chandler coined the
term. Chandler believed that 'down these mean streets a
man must go who is not himself mean'.

I'm not sure why I and another Jesuit student, Peter,
decided to make a pilgrimage from one side of Australia
to the other. Peter had joined the Jesuits the year after

me, also straight from school. Maybe we just had itchy feet and were looking for an adventure. But we were also serious about exploring the Ignatian tradition, as well as our own country. It was a preposterous idea: to cross the continent without a dollar to fall back on. The distance was 4500 kilometres. And the same back again. We'd walk parts of it and hitchhike other parts.

I remember the day I climbed the grand wooden staircase to go up to Brendan's office to see what he thought of the scheme. Given what had happened the previous summer at L'Arche, I thought he'd want me to spend this summer working somewhere he could keep an eye on me, in a parish perhaps. But to his credit, Brendan's immediate reaction was to jump up, go over to the railways map of Australia he had on his wall and start wondering where the road would take us. He was excited. There is no deeper form of trust than to be excited by someone else's dream.

I rang Mum and told her baldly what we were doing. I didn't tell her too much about anything in those days. Not long before this I had rung her to tell her not to bother coming down from Sydney to Melbourne for my twenty-first. The call was so brief that I had to ring back to tell her she could send the present if she wanted. My off-handedness was unintentionally cruel. But one of my reasons for taking the pilgrimage was to cut the apron strings good and proper. I could do something of which Mum thoroughly disapproved from within the safety of the sanction of St Ignatius himself. Call it dirty pool. She has never forgiven him. This was the occasion on which she came up with her now well-worn saying, that 'St Ignatius was never a mother.' I've heard it plenty of times since. It didn't stop me foraging under the house until I found a yellow ex-army webbing backpack in which I could fit a sleeping bag and two or three other items.

~

Peter and I set out on Boxing Day, 1983, from the Jesuit holiday house on the south coast of New South Wales, not far from where I'd been living with the L'Arche community. Christmas wrapping paper lined the road as we began to walk. Within ten kilometres we had blisters. Nothing like blisters to lance a quixotic dream. We were tired and grumpy before lunch on the first day's play. But when now I read over the diary I kept for the six weeks we were on the road, I am amazed at how we coped.

On our first night out, a farmer gave us shelter. We helped him load a Murray Grey bull onto a trailer. The bull was resisting a date with thirty cows. When we got home, the farmer's daughter and her recently divorced female friend tried to chat us up. We resisted more demurely than the Murray Grey. The next night another farmer let us sleep in an abandoned farmhouse which had been rocked by an earth tremor. He said it was unsafe. He told us not to complain to him if it fell on our heads and killed us. And not to tell other derelicts that he was a soft touch.

We got one of our first lifts with a bloke called Bluey who didn't so much drive his '62 Holden as do battle with it while his girlfriend, Jane, a ward of the state aged seventeen, sat silently in the passenger seat. Bluey was a carney, or carnival worker, one of Australia's band of itinerant sideshow attendants who traipse from one country show to the next. Bluey had a temper. He had walked out on a job in Kiama and was making for Horsham in an unregistered vehicle with half a tank of petrol. He decided to knock off a service station in Holbrook. That's when we parted company. Bluey wished us well. The next car that picked us up was an air-conditioned Mercedes. The driver gave us twenty dollars, 'because it's that time of year'. We put the money in the poor box and spent that night in Wodonga cemetery where we slept like the dead.

On New Year's Eve, we arrived in drenching rain at Nathalia, on the Murray. We were so desperate that we broke one of our rules and knocked on the presbytery door. The priest wasn't home. Later, he came looking for us downtown. He didn't know us from Adam but he'd already arranged for us to spend the night in the local pub and to eat at the cafe. The man who gave us a lift the following day was returning from the birth of his son at Yarrawonga hospital. That was how we saw in 1984. The world was teeming with life. A couple of years later, the priest who helped us, Les Ring, was killed in a car accident, probably caused by his own exhaustion. The town was numb with grief. I still measure my own response to the people who knock on our door against his.

We experienced human goodness as a kind of concentrate. Other people experience evil the same way. We were lucky.

One night we were swarmed by mosquitoes on the banks of the Murray. Our faces puffed up. Mosquitoes were causing a lot of disease on the Murray at the time. The following day we asked a fundamentalist minister if we could sleep in the relative safety of the caravan lurking in his carport.

In Mildura, an officious stalwart of the St Vincent de Paul gave us a speech about how he would have to stretch the rules to enable us to spend a night in a homeless shelter. But he did stretch them. There we were entertained by the other vagrants with stories of life on the road. One man told us that he was staying here because he'd been on a motorbike when a bee got in under his helmet. He managed to come safely to a stop but his face was swollen. Which meant that he couldn't get his helmet off until the swelling went down. Which meant he couldn't go into a bank to get money. Which meant he didn't have any choice but to camp at the homeless shelter. We believed him.

On the way to Renmark, a man gave us a lift on the condition that we helped him shovel a load of topsoil when we got there. After a while, he turned to look at us with what I thought was ominous intent. I feared the worst. Instead, he asked us toothlessly if we had ever heard of a figure called 'the black pope'. The Black Pope is a nickname sometimes given to the head of the Jesuit order, although the name hardly reflects the marginal position the order currently occupies in the temperamental culture of the Catholic Church. According to our host, this group called Jesuits were in league with Reagan, Marcos, Andropov and Thatcher to dominate the world. This was news to us. We kept mum, thinking that if we owned to being Jesuits at this stage, all his paranoid conspiracies would have been confirmed and his Christmases would have all come at once. But living in such a well-defended world didn't stop him offering hospitality to us and arranging for us to spend the night in the Baptist church. As we left the following day, he told us to be on the lookout for Jesuits. We said we'd write back if we saw any.

~

In all, we walked about 400 kilometres. We had some long waits for lifts. We decided not to leave Port Augusta, the last big town in South Australia before the Nullarbor Plain, until we could get a lift to the other side of the desert. There were no street lights after the last one in Port Augusta for another 2000 kilometres. We stood under that one, which is covered in graffiti left by our predecessors, for twenty-eight hours. We added some graffiti of our own. We were invisible to truck drivers who seemed to have no problem slamming on the air brakes when female hitchhikers were in the vicinity. The police took our details. Local hoons spat at us. Finally, an old station wagon lurched to a halt. It was hard to tell if it had stopped for us or had just chosen that spot to die.

'Where ya goan?'

'Perth.'

'You're laughing.'

We weren't laughing for long. Barney had bought the car the day before for $140. It was unregistered and the tyres were as bald as a statement. He was aboriginal. He had left school in Year 8. We had plenty of time to catch up on such details in the two days we spent together in the car. He told us that Nullarbor was an aboriginal name; we felt superior because we knew Latin.

Barney set a couple of rules for the trip. The first was

that he didn't want to stop more than was absolutely necessary because he was doubtful about the ignition on the car. Besides, he wanted a quick trip, to cross the country before he drew the attention of police. The second rule was somewhat in tension with the first. He didn't want to go more than 70 km/h for the 2500 kilometres because he only had ninety dollars and needed to conserve fuel. He was also worried about the engine blowing if we went too fast.

For two days, Peter and I survived on a packet of biscuits. We weren't worried about water: we could have lived off the sweat that gathered in pools where the springs in the vinyl seats had sagged. Strange to say, we really became fond of Barney, although he did give us some hair-raising moments. One of these was when we were overtaken by a motorbike gang. This was hardly surprising. At 70 km/h on the Nullarbor you feel like you are standing stock still. But Barney regarded being passed by bikies as a personal humiliation.

'Those motherfucking bastards,' he said, apparently describing the complex kinship system of bikie gangs. 'Moth-er-fuck-ers.'

Breaking his own rule, Barney stood on the accelerator and suddenly our $140 limousine shuddered into action. As we neared 90 km/h, it felt like it was going to take off. But eventually Barney managed to overhaul the motorbikes and settled complacently back to his normal speed. Before long, the bikes reappeared in the rear-vision mirror. Barney was spitting.

'Those arseholes,' he said. 'I'll wipe those arseholes.'

He told Peter, sitting in the back, to reach into the padding of the seat and pull out his Bowie knife.

'What do you want that for?'

Barney's plan was to hurl the knife into the back of one of the bike riders as he went past and bring him down. Our faces paled. Peter kept his wits about him and said he couldn't find the knife. He maintained the bluff for a few minutes until the gang was safely on its way. You don't notice too much of the arid beauty of the Nullarbor when you're travelling with Barney. But you feel close to Eyre, the first white to make the crossing, who was never too sure of making it in one piece.

Barney left us at Midlands on the outskirts of Perth. He had given us some loose change for good luck, so we went looking for a pub. We found one where there was a band playing, the Haloes; the band members got talking to us and one of them, Louie, offered us accommodation for the night on the floor of the room he occupied in a third-rate boarding house downtown. He spent the night smoking dope, but we did have the luxury of a shower, even if it was standing ankle deep in mould. In the morning, the slum landlord turned up to throw Louie onto the street for unpaid rent.

'I'm not going anywhere until I've given my guests breakfast,' he said.

It was his last night with a roof over his own head, but he had taken us in. I've never again heard of the Haloes. They weren't such a bad band.

~

We walked from Perth to New Norcia Abbey, our final destination. We had chosen it because of its remarkable place in history. It was about 130 kilometres and took us five more days. Our feet weren't coping well. A man with the evocative name of Tom Waters picked us up outside the gates of Bindoon, an institution about which we were to hear much more in the years ahead, for its role in the settlement of British children after World War II. Tom took us the last few miles, which was just as well because our strength was failing. Before buying us a beer at the New Norcia pub, he got us to sign the bonnet of his ute where our names joined those of dozens of others he had helped with lifts. Many of them, he said, had been picked up outside Bindoon. He also worked out his income tax on the same bonnet.

The rule of St Benedict urges hospitality to pilgrims, and the monks certainly lived up to the expectations of their founder. They took us away to recuperate at their secret hideout, an unserviced railway carriage which lies among the dunes on the coast south of Lancelin. God knows how it got there. But then God knows how we got there. As we stood watching the sun go down over the ocean in the west for the first time in our lives, I knew that a weight had been lifted from me, that I was looking at the scene without the cataracts of depression, that I could feel my feet, my toes and the breeze on my belly button.

I rang Mum reverse charges from a public phone to tell her we'd made it.

'That's great. Now when are you coming home?'

~

Shortly afterwards, we hitched a ride to Bunbury to visit the Catholic bishop who had stayed with us when we were novices. He took us out for Chinese. We told him our story and expected congratulations.

'How can you justify it?' he said immediately. He was quite angry. 'How can you justify doing what you did when half the world is starving and doesn't get any choice in the matter?'

It wasn't easy to answer. We had a strong sense on the road of being looked after, partly because we had chosen for a time to live with nothing. In five weeks, we had knocked on only one door which refused us food. Most people offered far more than we wanted. So, then, if God looked after us, why doesn't God look after the people who die of starvation every day? I can't answer that. But at least I can say that I have experienced that question as an unsettling riddle.

We talked a lot on the road. We talked about loneliness. About sex. About God. We read the Gospels to each other sitting in the dust by the side of the road. We sat in little old churches which had stood their ground for generations, like gnarled trees, on roadsides and in paddocks. We stopped in front of every one of the dozens of Anzac monuments we came across. In small communities, they might have half a dozen people listed on them, but three or four with the same surname. If we found a Catholic church, we waited for Mass, understanding a bit better why small groups of Christians huddle around simple gifts of bread and wine. We went into op-shops from time to time and begged for a change of clothes. We slept on beaches, in wheat fields, in parks, in sheds and garages, in derelict buildings. We got cranky and also had great fun. The result was a lasting friendship.

In the years ahead, Peter often took me more seriously than I was prepared to take myself. I am grateful to him for that. He left the priesthood soon after he was ordained because he had fallen in love. Before long, he had a family. I envied him. But celibacy, I reminded myself, is a choice to travel light, to possess nothing other than solitude. It presents God with a blank cheque, to sign or not as the case may be.

I have one precious souvenir of the pilgrimage. On our second day out, a couple insisted on giving us some tea-leaves to take with us. We explained that we didn't have a billy so they wouldn't be much use. In no time, Mr Bell had made a billy for us out of a long thin juice tin: he'd made it specifically to sit in the side pocket of my ex-army bag. He measured the pocket to make sure it would fit. Yet he was a complete stranger. That little billy, much blackened, sits on my bookshelf. It's funny that an object should come to embody so much of the experience of not having. But it does.

When I think of Dad, he is getting back into his truck. He has seen one of the nuns from school on the side of the road. She is walking towards the bus stop. She is carrying containers of Chinese takeaway. Chaussie food. Sweet and sour with chips. Beef with cashews and tomato sauce. Dad pulls over. He offers her a lift. She hasn't realised who he is. She accepts.

I am six. I am squirming. I have been in trouble with the nun for climbing onto the back fence at school and looking into the garden of the convent. The garden is where they have their washing line. But I didn't know that. I was in trouble, I realised, because a nun might have been hanging out her personal items. It was an act of God that I climbed the fence on an overcast day.

Dad opens the truck door for Sister. He is climbing back into his side. She sees me. She ignores me. Dad is smiling. He has a prisoner. He lambasts the nun for wasting the school fees on Chinese food. She tries to explain. It's a special day. A feast day. Dad says that only makes it worse. It's not fair. On her. I love it.

Three

IT WASN'T LONG AFTER Peter left the priesthood that I suggested to Mum that we go on a trip. By then I was realising how much we owed to ourselves.

So, twelve years after my first pilgrimage, Mum and I were browsing through the duty-free boutiques of Sydney International Airport. We loaded up with a watch, a camera, endless rolls of film, perfume, an electronic organiser and spirits. Basically, enough stuff so that if the plane went down, nobody would have to contend with the complexities of tidying up large legacies of cash. I also thought I'd buy a wallet.

'No need for a wallet,' said Mum firmly.

Shopping at the luxury goods end of the line is a bit like what I imagine it is to be on the Hollywood cocktail party circuit. You could be in any airport in the world; you could be in the shopping precinct of the Louvre; you could be in Venice. You keep running into the same tired old faces: Gucci, Oroton, Benetton, the Body Shop, Tie Rack, Virgin, Polo, Ralph Lauren. From time to time, they have face lifts and refits, but basically it's the same mob speaking the same clichés in every country of the world. At Sydney airport, you'd have been excused for wondering if I was the same man who had been happy to knock on doors for a piece of fruit or a sandwich. Sometimes, alcoholics will look back on a dry period as proof they can give up any time they want. Smokers the same. Or people who once lost a lot of weight in a short period will use that to fool themselves that their eating habits are just now in a period of aberration. But perhaps the period of self-control was the aberration. Maybe the pilgrimage was a time when my materialism was in a brief remission.

It's easy to be seduced. If you've ever wondered why you can't find the right book to read, it's because all the world's greatest writers are now doing advertising copy for perfume companies:

> *Woody and amber accents are enlivened by fresh, light florals and the surprise counterpoint of balsamic notes, to achieve an eau de toilette with fullness and clarity.*
> *A clean scent energised with citrus, mint and a crisp sea breeze accord, enhanced by masculine fresh florals and woody notes.*

Somebody must take this stuff seriously. At sixty and eighty bucks a capful, they ought to. Luckily, Mum, a pharmacist, comes from a world in which perfume is handled by shop assistants. For all the purple prose in the world, the four words 'take twice a day' carry more weight in her mind.

> *This highly sensual fragrance blends warm oriental notes with essences of amber, vanilla, orchid*

and rose, to redefine femininity and celebrate the beauty of woman.

I was still reading these blurbs in the inflight catalogue when we landed at Heathrow. Mum touched me on the arm as the plane taxied. She had something to say.

'My father never came back here,' she said. She was referring to John Baxter, a man I never met. 'He never returned to England. Once he left, that was it.'

I picked up the magazine again.

'And he took nothing with him,' she said. 'Not a thing.'

My aunt, Trixie, and her husband Kevin met us at the airport.

'My God, you've brought enough stuff,' she said, loading our cases into her little car.

Trixie had waited years for Mum's arrival. She was actually Dad's sister but Mum and Trixie had started school together and have been life-long friends. No sooner were we in the car than she told the story of the mattress she had bought for Mum and Dad's arrival in 1959. She had kept it for twenty years before finally getting rid of it. She didn't say as much, but it was in 1979 that Dad died.

'We live opposite that little shop there,' said Kevin, Trixie's husband.

The little shop was Harrods.

During breakfast, Kevin looked up from his watch at ten o'clock and announced that Harrods was now open for business. The comment was wry. But it wasn't long before I realised that the whole family is struck from the same stock. Trixie and Kevin live in a house which is so replete with the accumulation of years that it makes the Victoria and Albert Museum, Britain's national attic, look like Zen minimalism. Trixie is a member of the House of Lords. Her baronial motto is 'Keep going'. It could just as easily be 'Keep everything'. In her upstairs bedroom she has her own personal shrine to the Things You Get For Free. On the bath shelf is an enormous glass vat, the size of a modest Egyptian tomb. This vat is brimful of the small wrapped soaps you get in hotels and which Trixie has brought back from every corner of the globe. You could make an interesting study of cross-cultural habits of personal hygiene. You could also study, stratum by stratum, the changing nature of complimentary soap through the ages.

Mum and Trixie have an accumulation of memories which is softer than soap. Within minutes of the teapot hitting the table, they were roaming freely across the sixty-five years of their friendship. Names budded from nowhere. The fortunes and misfortunes of people I'd never heard of were discussed with passion.

Trixie confided that she did not even have a picture of her own mother. Trixie must also have mentioned this in a postcard at some stage. Now Mum went to the suitcase with wheels and worked her way into one of the secret zippered compartments. Triumphantly, she produced a photo of Trixie and her mother standing together in King Street, Sydney, in 1943. It was taken across the street from the pharmacy in which Mum worked at the time. Trixie was delighted.

Four

I OWE A LOT TO TRIXIE. It was because of her that Mum and Dad got together in the first place. Mum and Dad met, dated and married in a world that scarcely still exists.

One weekend in Sydney, Mum's parents, Linda and John Baxter, were supposed to go to a function at the Seafarers' Club, a mission to travellers run by the church. Most ports had a flourishing Seamen's Mission. Many still do. Its main purpose was to provide enough entertainment to keep lonely crew members out of brothels. Mum's mother took sick and asked Mum to go along in her place. Mum was understandably not too keen. Apart from the fact that Mum worked six days a week and Sunday afternoon was virtually her only time to herself, I can't imagine the prospect of socialising with sailors who'd come ashore for the first time in weeks was all that appealing. Most of them were covered in tattoos. Mum hates tattoos. But my grandmother insisted because she owed a favour to a priest called Father Donovan who was organising the event and she couldn't let him down.

At the function, Maureen Baxter found herself sitting alongside one Greg McGirr. I'm not sure why Dad was there. He never went to sea and certainly had no interest in sailors, tattooed or otherwise. But he had been to the races the day before and lost money, so perhaps he had nowhere else to go on a quiet Sunday. More likely he was drawn by the prospect of doing somebody a good turn. He was an impossibly generous man. I suspect he saw his turbulent gambling career as a form of charity to bookmakers. He may not have had two coins to rub together on that particular Sunday, but the seafarers were raising money so Dad got into his truck and turned up.

Greg introduced himself to Maureen who immediately asked if he was any relation to Trixie McGirr, with whom she'd been at school. Trixie had gone overseas to find fame, fortune and love a few years before. Dad said Trixie was his sister and that she was coming out from England the following week. Would Mum care to come to a function they were holding for her? The function was to be at Sydney's famous Trocadero ballroom. Mum accepted. Dad arrived to pick her up in a cantankerous Chevrolet utility truck. Mum had not bargained on the truck.

Dad had bought his truck in 1946, twelve years before, when he was twenty. Vehicles were in short supply after World War II – you had to go into a ballot for the right to buy one. Dad was helped, however, by the fact that he was a farmer and primary industries got a preference. That truck was a sign of Dad's independence; he became dependent on it.

When Mum climbed up into the cab in her ball gown

to go to the Trocadero, the truck was already the worse for wear. The upholstery was impregnated with the dust of many trips up bush. On the seat, between the pair of them, was Dad's Gladstone bag. Dad was a great believer in getting value out of anything he paid for. The Gladstone bag was an example. It was small, made of leather and steel-framed. It was so heavy that these days you'd be paying excess baggage even if it was empty. Dad got the bag when, at his father's instigation, he was sent away to agricultural school. According to Trixie, my grandfather didn't put a lot of thought into Dad's future. He just decided that it would be good to have an agriculturalist in the family and enrolled him in Hawkesbury Agricultural College. Dad was fine with the academic curriculum but not at all cut out for the wear and tear of life on the land. Every Sunday night when Dad returned to the college from North Sydney, his Gladstone bag contained freshly laundered shirts, more suited for a public servant, and a bar of Cadbury chocolate which he divided up and rationed to last the week.

I don't know why he needed the Gladstone bag on the first date with Mum. He didn't have a job at the time. He sometimes carried the bag around empty. It was a fixture in Dad's sparsely furnished world.

The truck's steering was only ever approximate and Mum had to reach across the bag and hold the truck in gear while Dad reversed out of the drive. Mum's father, John Baxter, who had been unwell, stayed inside listening suspiciously to the engine and just hoping Dad wouldn't back over his beloved garden.

By the time they turned the first corner, Mum was

already worried about her dry-cleaning bill. She thought that the truck was on its last legs. She was wrong. It started the evening as the love of Dad's life. It soon became his second love and lasted until twelve months before he died.

~

Like most of Australia's great dance venues the Trocadero is now defunct. When it closed, it was the Jesuits, ironically, who bought its leftover crockery. Heaven knows how this transaction came about, but when I was a novice I ate three meals a day from the plates that Mum and Dad had placed before them on their first date. They were trimmed in maroon and finished with a pair of dancers lost in the wonder of each other. Over the course of the two-year novitiate, I had plenty of opportunity to envy those figures. Those plates were utterly unbreakable, designed to withstand both the impact of an angry stiletto and the washing-up habits of clumsy novices, so I can be sure they were the same ones. If the Trocadero seemed like a lifetime away from the novitiate, I could console myself that in my case it literally was.

~

Four or five months after the ball at the Troc, Dad dropped in on Mum at the Crown Street Hospital where she worked in the pharmacy. He noticed that Mum was wearing an engagement ring. He was taken aback. Maybe some other bloke had beaten him to the punch. Mum explained that it was the engagement ring of her mother, who had died shortly before, and that she only wore it for safe keeping.

'What kind of ring do you like, Maureen?' he asked.

'I think I like a single stone,' replied Mum.

It dawned on Mum later that this was Dad's proposal of marriage. When the ring arrived, it dawned on her that she must have accepted.

They announced their engagement after Christmas Midnight Mass at the Seafarers' Club. The first person they told was the priest, Father Donovan. I wonder what Donovan thought of the prospects of a couple who'd known each other only six months. I once married a couple who wanted to have the U2 song 'I still haven't found what I'm looking for' played as they left the church. I told them that this would be a bit like having 'It's all over now, baby blue'. They said they didn't mind 'Baby Blue' and might have that as well. But the couple has remained happily together, so you can't judge too hastily. I have heard of couples wanting 'Desperado' and 'Only the lonely'. Even so, the priest may have wondered why Greg was so difficult and kept changing the time for the rehearsal of the wedding. One of Greg's sisters, Muffie, took him to task and told him to get his act together. Still, the priest may also have wondered why Maureen was so determined to be married on the Feast of Our Lady of Perpetual Succour.

When Mum got to the altar on her wedding day, Dad looked her anxiously in the shins. He had noticed, as she came down the aisle, that the dress she had chosen was layered at the front, according to the fashion of the day, and revealed enough of the bride's legs for him to be embarrassed. The hem hung at the giddy height of fifteen inches from the ground. Mum had never played soccer and wasn't interested in cards, the two sports in

which you get kicked in the shins, so there was no reason why she shouldn't show off the fact that hers were
in good repair. But Mum and Dad had had a modest
courtship, so much so that Dad was unprepared for the
sight of his bride's ankle as she came down the aisle. Dad
was not the type to keep his thoughts to himself. Nor
any judge of an occasion.

'For God's sake,' he said when Mum finally took him
by the arm, 'pull your dress down at the front.'

There are special occasions – weddings, funerals and
when you get pulled over by the police – on which you
can say things that can never be unsaid. Mum was hurt.
Those words reverberated throughout their marriage.

Dad's reserve on all matters pertaining to the flesh
was legendary, even among his sisters. He once
described a record of Beethoven sonatas on sale at a
fete as 'lewd' because there was a Botticelli painting on
the cover featuring a chaste-looking but bare-breasted
woman. Yet he was a devotee of World Championship
Wrestling and, coming home from Mass on Sunday
morning, he'd be happily entertained by the antics of
Brute Barnard and Mario Milano for the time it took
Mum to get his baked dinner ready. When my brother
and I were entering our teenage years, he took a close
interest in the modesty of our swimming costumes. He
didn't want to see us dressed like Mario and Brute.
Another time, he was angry because Mum had given
advice within our earshot to a young couple who were
trying to conceive a child. She told them to stop trying
so hard and 'just let it happen'. I was once watching 'A
Current Affair' on TV with Dad and heard the word
'rape'. I asked Dad what it meant. He couldn't bring

himself to tell me. Mum and Dad said the rosary when they went to bed. They were very good. Even for the times.

~

On the day after the wedding, Mum and Dad had their photo in the *Sun-Herald*. They are announced to the world as 'Mr and Mrs Gregory McGirr' and then, with sudden finality, come the words 'the bride was formerly Miss Maureen Baxter.' Opposite the picture of the happy couple is an advertisement for a sewing machine for 39 guineas; an earlier page has TVs for 129 guineas and Kelvinator refrigerators, looking like the front end of a Dodge, for 104 guineas. A laminex kitchen table and matching chairs, trimmed with vinyl tubing, were 17 guineas. Looking through the ads, you notice the big Sydney retailers – Nock & Kirby, Mark Foy's, Anthony Horderns and Waltons – all a thing of the past. So is much else. It was a religiously secure, if narrow, world. Because it was a Sunday paper, there's a religious reflection. That week's was about eternal life; the Reverend Dr Malcolm Mackay was a stranger to inclusive language:

> *Surely modern man, of all mankind, ought to agree that behaviour and morals are not just concocted to suit the moment, but belong to the realm of the absolute and final things.*

Cardinal Gilroy was equally sure where he stood. He was the subject of a news story. At the very moment Mum and Dad were getting married, Gilroy was opening a convent in Bankstown. The twelve Josephite nuns who were going to live in it would be the teaching staff of a new school in a growing area. Gilroy was secure enough among his own people, within his own sub-culture, to joke about debt, always a more tricky subject of humour than sex, even for a Cardinal.

'I am amazed at the progress that has taken place in the parish,' said Gilroy. 'When you came here you had a miserable debt of £6,500 – a mere nothing at all. Now you are able to boast a debt of £20,000.'

In an hour an a half, the function raised £1300 to house the sisters. By that time, Dad had made his *faux pas* about the dress, the driver of the wedding car had asked if anybody knew where they were meant to be going, and Mum had said I do. They were going to her home at Mowbray Road to pay their respects to Mr Baxter. Then to breakfast. Then to Brisbane for a few days. The *Sunday Mirror* reported that *from there they will leave during the week for a three months' honeymoon in Europe.* The *Catholic Weekly*, then, as now, ahead of the times, said, *after flying to Brisbane, the newly weds left by ship for an overseas trip.* This was not quite true. They didn't get any further than Brisbane. Audrey Hepburn was the one who had the Roman Holiday, even if hers only lasted a day. In her wedding photos, Mum looks a bit like Hepburn. Especially her hair. It was the style.

~

John Baxter had been unwell and was not able to come to the church. A cousin, Jack Morris, had volunteered to spend the morning with him so he would not be entirely on his own. Once Mum settled down, John was going to be alone in the house, but he was not a man who showed emotion readily, least of all self-pity. Not long before the wedding he had found his wife, Linda, in the garden after she had suffered a heart attack. He carried her back to the house. His only comment on the silent world of his widowhood was that now he could sometimes hear the workers singing while they were building the Channel Nine TV tower, which was going up not far away. When the bridal party arrived on June 27, he had difficulty standing to greet them. In better days, John Baxter had made the chair he was sitting in. He had made every piece of furniture in the room. Now he had trouble shaking hands.

John's sickness had developed not long after his wife died, a few weeks before the wedding. Lung cancer. It was the first reason the honeymoon was delayed. He was a marine engineer in the merchant navy, came from Newcastle-on-Tyne and had been smoking since he was nine. In a way, he was lucky to make it to his seventies. Mum can't remember what brand he used to smoke, only that he used to roll his own. She has never liked smoking. In fact, she loathes and detests it. Mum always expresses displeasure in duplicate. She never talks about dishonest politicians, only filthy stinking ones. For her, smoking is a dirty and disgusting habit. I once asked her if her father had tattoos. Being in the navy and all that. I thought it likely, especially in the days before tattoos became trendy.

'He'd never do anything so common and repulsive.'

Mum's father died in September. One Saturday after the wedding Mum had been visiting her father in hospital.

He told her to take the paper with her when she went. She didn't want the paper. He insisted. She took it just to keep him happy.

At this stage, Mum and Dad were alternating between living at 'her' place and living at 'his', meaning, of course, their parents' places. They were sleeping on the folding divan which Mum still has in the lounge room at home. My elder brother has cause to be grateful to that divan.

Mum and Dad had looked at a flat in Cronulla and a bungalow in Katoomba, both places miles and miles from the centre of town. This was their price range. Mum had already saved up and bought a little land in the Blue Mountains.

On their walks together they had eyed off the houses they liked, and one in particular. Mum liked it because it was Federation brick-on-sandstone. Dad liked it because the current owners had the poor taste to paint the woodwork crimson. There was also room for a dog. That very house was advertised for sale in the paper Mum's father had forced on her. They decided to stretch their finances. It was certainly the end of the overseas trip.

~

Mum believes that everything happens for a purpose. If she can't find a car park, it's because, for some inexplicable reason, she's not 'meant' to buy what she came out to get and, before long, she's found the reason why she's better off without it. Growing up, the story of the house was often produced as evidence for the same belief.

'If we hadn't missed the trip, we would never have got the house.'

I often suspected that Mum was talking about something deeper.

'If my father hadn't died when he did, we might never have got the house,' was what she wasn't saying.

Both Mum's parents and her only sister died in a period of eight years. By 1966, her immediate family had all gone. She kept busy. She made a nest. She protected her three children.

It's understandable that we heard so much more about Dad's family. They were more numerous and more exotic. A number had rumbustious political careers. Besides, Mum is the type to cover her wounds with stockings and even, on the rare nights she had out with Dad, with elbow-length gloves. She spent the whole of the sixties renovating the inside of the house while Dad watched from the foot of the ladder, occasionally pointing out places where the paint had been applied a bit too thin. She's the only person I've met from her age group who can't remember where she was when Kennedy was shot. She missed Sydney's record earth tremor because she was standing over a twin-tub washing machine which shuddered like that all the time anyway. The only comment she ever made about menopause was that she didn't have time for it.

~

Mum's world was largely defined by the house. To this day, she loves it when real estate agents leave cards in her letterbox offering to buy the place. She will say exactly what she thinks it is worth, to the dollar, and then announce that she has no intention of ever selling. She will tell you, within days of a sale, what any place nearby 'went for'.

We were a stay-at-home family. I read a lot of Mum's travel literature and could have told you that Timbuktu was in Mali, but I would have had trouble recognising the faces of the people next door. During winter, we lived in the small kitchen which Mum heated by lighting the gas oven and leaving its door ajar. Our clothes were draped over the door of the oven to dry. Five times during the summers when we were little, bushfires came roaring up the gully to within feet of the front door. The only one I can remember, in 1969, was brought to our attention by Mr MacDonald who lived next door. Mum was so caught up with getting a meal on the table for the three kids that she hadn't even noticed that the entire suburb was thick with smoke. Indeed, it was so rare for a neighbour to call that his sudden appearance in shorts and a beard was initially met with some indignation, until the flames at his back made it clear he had a reasonable pretext. For months after the last fire, the one we had to drive through to get out of our driveway to safety, I kept all my precious belongings in a chocolate tin which sat inside a vinyl valise on top of my bed: my textas, my padlock, my penknife, my brand new first communion medal. Just in case there was another fire, I could grab the lot when we had to run.

There were times when Mum nearly took her trip. When the last of us left school, when Dad died, when Trixie was elevated to the House of Lords. Always, however, there was something else. I don't know how many times I heard 'if I ever go overseas'. Dad died, my brother left home and I went off to become a priest in a space of about twelve months. That left Mum and my sister, in the middle of high school, still at home. Mum's response to the empty-nest syndrome was the opposite of normal. It was, however, what her father might well have done in the circumstances. She decided to extend the house. She added a huge room to accommodate a ping-pong table. This room had first been proposed when it looked like we might need to set up a kidney machine for Dad at home. Now, said Mum, we needed the same facility for table tennis. The table cost $149. The addition cost $25,000. I'm not sure if anyone has ever actually played ping-pong on it. But here was Mum saying loud and clear that her home was her world. The day I left home, they poured the foundations.

Five

WE DID THE TOURIST TRAIL IN LONDON. We bought things we didn't really want and carefully filled in the forms to get back the tax we paid on them when we left the country. I dragged Mum to literary shrines: we went to Dr Johnson's house and squandered time in the book shops in Charing Cross Road. We also happened to wander past the Royal Courts of Justice just when Bob Geldof and Paula Yates were inside sorting out their famously unhappy relationship. There was an encampment of paparazzi outside waiting to get another shot of Yates's tattoos, which were said to change colour with her mood. The paparazzi were indignant when I tried to take a photo of them. They were jealous of their privacy.

We saw the names of some of my Jesuit forebears carved into the stone at the Tower of London. For Mum, the Reformation was yesterday. Every church we went to was either 'ours' or 'theirs'. St Paul's was one of 'theirs'. We were standing on the spot where Charles and Diana had pledged their undying love when a procession of men and women in surplices and gowns went past bearing candles. A few minutes later they returned without the candles. The last person in the procession now had a mobile phone clasped to her ear. Perhaps she was talking to God.

'Anglicans,' said Mum, as if that explained it.

It was in one of 'their' places, Westminster Abbey, that we began to realise the significance of what Craig had said about crowds. Tour groups moved through each other like swarms of fish. On the hour, a voice on the PA tried to restore a minute's calm in token recognition of the fact that this is supposed to be a church and not Disneyland. The voice then led a recitation of the Lord's Prayer, which infuriated Mum because the voice said, 'Our father, which art in heaven' instead of 'who art in heaven'. I told her it was better than the Andy Warhol version, 'Our pop art in heaven.'

In Poets' Corner, you can hear every language, even English. A Chinese guide pointed to the monument to Handel and hummed a few bars of the *Messiah*. Her group nodded in recognition. A Spanish guide pointed at the monument to the poet Gerard Manley Hopkins and said, '*Era un sacerdote jesuita.*' The Italian guide pointed to T.S. Eliot and said something about *la commedia cats*. A cockney guide drew attention to Browning's monument. She was outraged that Browning's wife, Elizabeth Barrett Browning, had been interred in Italy. She hoped some Italian of letters, say Umberto Eco, would die in England so they could do an exchange of their remains. She told her group that Dylan Thomas was a lewd man who wrote beautiful stuff whereas D.H. Lawrence just wrote lewd stuff. We paid our respects at the monument to Adam Lindsay Gordon, one of our locals.

The abbey is completely overgrown with history. It is cluttered with tombs and monuments honouring history-makers. But I go along with Tolstoy's theory that it's not the Napoleon Bonapartes who change the course of lives but the people you've never heard of. Suddenly, Mum produced some evidence for this theory. She told me, out of the blue, that her mother had been engaged to a fellow who had been killed in France during World War I. His name was Bader, the son of a Canon Bader. Perhaps it was being in an Anglican church that put Mum in mind of this. At Crown Street Women's Hospital, Mum had worked alongside one of Bader's relatives, the nephew of the man who could have been her father. But that was not to be.

On the day I was ordained a Catholic priest, Mum gave me the pair of cuff-links which her mother had given her father on their wedding day. They are a precious possession. I love them because they are my only link with her parents. They are inscribed with the date of the marriage in September, 1918. They were married, in other words, before the end of the war which had claimed Linda's first fiancé.

'I didn't know that,' I said to Mum as we left the Abbey.

She apologised.

'There's a lot in my family I don't talk about,' she said.

Dad is getting into his truck. He has the three kids for the day. Mum has gone away for the funeral of a relative, someone 'on her side'. He takes us for Chinese food and talks to his mate at the service station next to the restaurant. They talk for ages. My sister dirties her nappy. Dad can't stand the smell. He puts her on the tray of the truck with her two brothers to look after her. He gets back into the cab and waves to us happily through the back window. He drives around town until he knows Mum will be home to change the nappy. He doesn't know what else to do. He tells her we were good as gold.

Six

TRIXIE IS ALSO Baroness Gardner of Parkes. She was made a life peer when I was a novice. Around the same time, her eldest daughter was diagnosed with multiple sclerosis. Trixie deals with both triumph and tragedy in the same practical spirit. Mrs Thatcher put her into the Lords, I understand, because Trixie had won ground for the Tories by standing in difficult seats in elections during the seventies and because of her work on the Greater London Council. But the job was more than grace and favour. Trixie is committed to serving the reality in which Mrs Thatcher did not believe – society. She soon fell out with Thatcher over cuts to the National Health Service, especially in the area of dentistry, when Trixie managed to organise the government to defeat its own bill on the floor of the upper house. Gardner of Parkes sounds like Forrest of Trees or Baker of Bred, but her title comes from Parkes, New South Wales. This is where the McGirrs originate in Australia and from where my grandfather and his two brothers began their colourful careers as Labor politicians in the first decades of the twentieth century.

Trixie treated us to lunch in the peers' dining room at the House of Lords. It's a pity this event is not on the tourist circuit. Trixie told us of the days in which a famous tea house employed actors to pretend to be Messrs Fortnum & Mason and drink tea in the shop all day. I don't see why they shouldn't employ actors to perform as peers. It would be a hit. Trixie thinks that rather than remarry, widowers should all be raised to a peerage and become members of the House of Lords.

'It's the perfect place for them. They're not quite there for breakfast but certainly come in well before lunch. If there's business in the house, they may stay on for dinner and get a cab home. And they get all the nursery food they love. Rice puddings and all that stuff.'

The cook in the peers' dining room once confessed to Trixie that he had begun to cut the fat off the lamb cutlets but this had unleashed a storm around his ears. He had never had so many complaints about anything. And he was in no position to retort that he was trimming the fat for health reasons, because all the complainants were well past average life expectancy.

I hand it to my aunt. That day, she was moving on any number of fronts. She was taking a large part in debating a key item of housing legislation as well as being responsible for the passage through the upper house of a noise reduction bill. Yet, in the middle of all that, she looked up from her Dover Sole and asked Kevin, her husband, whether or not you turn this kind of fish or if you pull out the skeleton. Kevin explained this was the difference between a Dover Sole and a Lemon Sole: what you did with the backbone. The things you learn.

At 3 p.m., the House sat. The instructions for sitting

are known as 'standing orders'. By this stage of the after-noon, many of the noble Lords, gallant dukes and right reverend prelates had gone to the library, turned their chairs to the wall and picked up where they had left off from yesterday's siesta. The House of Lords does have a kind of egalitarianism. They all bunk in together for their sleep in the library. They all have to share offices. Unless they are entertaining, they are expected to sit at lunch with any old body. The only thing they have to call their own is their coat-hook inside the front door. The Prince of Wales' coat-hook is no more impressive than my aunt's. Nor is Baroness Thatcher's. People speak of going 'up' to the Lords, but it must have been a considerable comedown to move from 10 Downing Street to a mere coat-hook. You can buy those coat-hooks at Boots' pharmacies for a quid. We knew that. In between appointments at the Lords, we had been inspecting pharmacies on this side of the world.

Before long, a division was called. It seemed cruel to me to disturb the peers from their siesta. We watched them file in on sticks and crutches. They voted and went back to bed.

In the foyer outside, Mum told me how proud she was.

'I've known Trixie since she was that high,' she said, pointing obliviously to the knee of the Deputy Prime Minister. He was on his way to somewhere else and so were we.

Seven

WE COULD HARDLY get our suitcases into the tiny white Vauxhall we had rented to drive around Britain. But we managed somehow and then squeezed into the front seats. Our shoulders were practically touching. We were going to spend a lot of time close together. This made us a little wary and edgy. We talked wantonly about things like the cost of fuel, but we measured our confidences.

A few weeks later we would be on our conducted bus tour of Italy. For ten days, we were to have the pleasure of being the only people on a list of forty-two who did not come from the United States. This made for a lot of fun. But there proved to be a culture gap, especially when members of the tour started coming to the front of the bus to give their life stories through the microphone. We rolled through the beautiful fields of Tuscany as a travelling studio audience for Oprah Winfrey or Jerry Springer. One woman lurched up the centre aisle and began by saying that she supposed we'd all been wondering about the man she was travelling with and herself. We had been doing nothing of the sort.

'I have to tell you that we are not married.'

She expected a gasp.

'We were married once. But the relationship was getting stale. We both come from very strict backgrounds. So we decided to put some of the spice back into life by getting divorced and living in sin together.'

Mum needed tissues to dab away the tears of laughter that were smudging her make-up.

The next woman to get up announced that she and her husband had been married for twenty-five years. This brought a polite round of applause.

'But I have to tell you, the relationship is not going so well. This is our make it or break it tour.'

Ian, the teenage son who was travelling with them, turned all the colours of a Tuscan sunset.

'We'll keep you posted on how things are going throughout the tour,' said Tess as she signed off for now.

'No thanks,' said Mum, barely audible.

The regular posting actually involved the couple flirting with virtually everyone on the bus for the whole ten days in the hope that one of them could make the other jealous. They couldn't. They could only make the rest of us squirm. On the final night of the tour, the guide took us to the Trevi Fountain in Rome. He announced that if you threw in a coin, you would return to Rome someday. I held on to my money, as Rome is one place for a priest to avoid for any purpose other than a holiday. The guide said that if you threw in two coins you'd come back married and if you threw in three coins you'd come back divorced. The couple on the make-it-or-break-it tour started scrounging around for loose change. They each threw in a small fortune, almost the price of a cup of coffee in Rome. So I guess they didn't make it.

The funny thing was that these people seemed to be only able to cope with intimacy in the realm of public performance. You couldn't shut them up when they had a sizeable audience, but they were virtually impossible to engage in conversation otherwise. I concluded they were actually private people for whom life had to feel like it was taking place on television for it to feel safe. Many of them sat glued to CNN all night long in their hotel rooms, 'just to keep in touch'. They kept so much in touch that they slept during the day and seldom got off the bus. They saw Italy behind a glass screen.

~

Mum and I are not like that. We are private as well. But our privacy looks private. Being in a car together for two weeks did not necessarily mean we'd talk at length about ourselves across the breadth of Britain. But we were alive to each other's every mood and reaction.

The front of the car is our place for confidences. People point out that this is typical of the reserve of Australian men. When they have something to say, they get side by side. So they talk standing at the bar, at a workbench in the much-celebrated backyard shed, or next to each other at a sports event. The reason, I suppose, is that we don't have to cope with eye contact.

I had been sitting in the front of a car with Mum just like this when I told her I was going to join the Jesuits. I was seventeen. We were on the Sydney Harbour Bridge at the time. Mum was dropping me in to the Opera House to hear a lecture on *Great Expectations*, one of the novels we were studying for the Higher School Certificate. I've kept the ticket as a memento: Sunday,

July 1, 1979. Mum was caught entirely unawares and thrown off guard. We got to the toll booth and she rolled down the window to pay the money.

'How long have you been thinking about this?' she asked the collector.

I'd been thinking about it for a week. I was in my last year at school. Mid-year, our school had offered us the chance to go away to the Jesuit novitiate for a three-day retreat. There wasn't much response because the year before our whole class had been dragged away on a Christian Living Camp. I never understood the name, as there wasn't much Christian living done on those camps. I was, I suppose, an insecure agnostic by this stage and the form smart arse to boot but, when I saw only a handful were interested, I grabbed the chance with both hands because at least it would mean a few days away from home and school. I was finding my final year a dispiriting experience and had had a huge fight with Dad when my term results were below par. I did not realise at the time how sick he had become and therefore how desperate. We were both insensitive to the precipices we had reached in our respective lives; we didn't have too many clues about how to talk to each other without trying to draw blood.

I'm not sure what happened during those three days. I sat still. A priest who knew me as a kid told me, in a way I could hear, that I'd become arrogant. I told him about Dad. I cried. I felt a weight lifting. I felt happy. When we finished talking, I asked to see a room where the novices lived. I didn't know it, but I had already decided to join the Jesuits. I'm not sure I could even spell the word. I cried more then than I did three months later when Dad died. I had uncovered my tender side and with that I uncovered an ability to believe in God.

'It's funny,' Mum said, sitting in the car at the bridge toll booth. 'Father Donovan said that your father's sickness would end in a vocation.'

~

Not long after Dad's funeral, Mum and I were once again going some place in the car.

'Are you still thinking of joining the Jesuits next year?'

The topic hadn't come up in the meantime. I had never mentioned it to Dad.

'Yes, I am.'

'Why don't you do a degree first?'

'I don't think I will.'

'You might need.'

'Go on.'

'You might need something to fall back on.'

'Maybe.'

That was as far as I was prepared to discuss it.

God knows what was really going on. Maybe I wanted to run away from home and had lighted on the only escape clause which would cost me nothing and about which Mum, a devout Catholic, could hardly complain. I'm surprised that nobody saw through me. Perhaps they did and I was not prepared to listen. My slipping away from a grieving family was the kind of behaviour you might expect from a teenager who thought at the time that he'd finalised adolescence when the bands came off his teeth and he'd had his first row with a girl. In fact, I hadn't even begun.

I only wonder now that unpromising beginnings

should have opened up for me such a happy life. I don't use the word lightly, but I believe I have been blessed. I am learning painfully how to like myself and allow myself to hunger for God. But that has taken time. And distance.

By then, at seventeen, I had become skilled at finding places to hide. One of them was literature. During several long summer holidays, when Dad was sick and Mum was working, I would do a delivery round in the early morning and sell papers on North Sydney Station in the afternoon. I had been there on the station on the day the tabloids produced special editions to cover the Granville rail disaster, in which dozens of people were killed on their way to work. I remember ducking into a book shop to look up in a dictionary the meaning of the word 'carnage' which was draped in huge letters across the front page. More importantly, I remember how people who bought the special editions were visibly distressed. All of them had caught the train to work that day themselves. But they stood apart from each other, reading, then continued in silence downstairs to the train platforms. That troubled me. I wondered why nobody wanted to discuss the news, why people needed to be isolated at such a moment.

I was spending most of the time in between delivering morning papers and selling afternoon papers at home, reading. I read most of Dickens. Austen. Waugh. Greene. Piles of stuff. I didn't just read it, I somehow vanished inside it. Swapped places with the characters. Unconsciously, on this side of the text, the real side, I began impersonating characters such as Pickwick and Micawber. People laughed. But unobserved by anyone, on the other side of the text, the safe side, characters began impersonating me. I spoke to these friends about the things I felt and the problems I had.

This was fine, up to a point. The point was clear a few weeks after I finished school.

~

I had just got my driver's licence. On Saturday mornings I used to go with a friend to help out on what was called Dawn Patrol, a service which used to take coffee and sandwiches around to people who'd been sleeping out overnight in parks, doorways and under bridges. It was challenging work. We met all types, some of them younger than ourselves. We started work about 5 a.m. and I used to pick up a friend called Paul on the way.

One day, we were heading along the Pacific Highway towards the city in the first light of dawn. I was a bit sleepy, and changed lanes carelessly.

I remember time inching forward frame by frame. I saw the first car hit us. Then a second.

Three cars ended up in a tangled mess against a telegraph pole at Artarmon. If that pole had not caught us, we would all have been killed.

Paul was badly injured. His blood was everywhere. I remember deciding, before the ambulances arrived, that Paul would be OK.

Dad had died not long before and my only experience of a dead body was that it was clean and orderly. Not like this. All three vehicles were written off, including my brother's car. Paul did recover, but carried an ugly scar deep in his forehead. He grew his fringe long to cover it. I remember as he was taken away in the ambulance, one of the local residents asked me if I was OK. I certainly was not. But all I could find to say were the words of Pip in *Great Expectations* when he realises he has hurt his guardian, Joe. We'd studied the book at school and I knew it cover to cover. I thanked the stranger, in the words of Joe Gargery, for being a 'gentle Christian man'. The stranger looked at me like I was from outer space.

I could step out of reality almost at will.

Later that afternoon, I went with my brother to visit the remains of his car. We looked at it in disbelief, wondering how anybody could have got out alive. My brother was remarkably easygoing about the loss. His main concern was to get something out of the boot before the car was sent for scrap. What he wanted to rescue was the present he'd bought me for going away to join the Jesuits. It was a travelling bag.

~

I arrived at the Jesuit novitiate at the same time as a fellow novice, a young Vietnamese, who came with all his possessions in a single drawstring shopping bag. He was one of the wave of boat people who came to Australia in the late seventies, and hardly spoke three sentences of English. I, on the other hand, had two enormous suitcases and some smaller bags as well, including the one my brother had given me. I had packed such necessities of the ascetic life as a hair dryer and a full range of Brut 33 toiletries. Brut 33 may have been the ubiquitous smell of Australia in 1980 but it was unfamiliar in the Jesuit noviceship. Luckily, when Phong and I had our luggage piled up in the hall together, it looked like a reasonable amount of stuff for two people.

It wasn't an easy occasion, least of all for Mum. There were some pleasantries with the novice master and the other novices, before I went out to the car to say goodbye. I didn't know what to say. So I started quoting from Donne's poem, 'A Valediction Forbidding Mourning'. I can still run it out from memory.

'So let us part and make no noise.'

I think Mum was a bit stunned.

'No tear floods nor sigh tempests move.'

I didn't want a scene.

A few weeks later I had a letter from my brother in which he said he had sat beside Mum in the car on the way home. She had cried the whole distance. According to long Jesuit tradition, joining the order is a decisive break with any previous existence. It was seven years before I spent a night at home again. By that time I'd slept in parks, cemeteries and on beaches and was ready to concede that home had its advantages.

~

Eight years after I joined the Jesuits, in 1988, my brother and his best friend, Kerin, got married. I was back in Sydney, teaching in a boarding school which the Jesuits ran. Mum drove me home. We were in the front of the car again. We got talking about the wedding and what various people had said and worn and all that sort of stuff. I was pleasantly tipsy.

'You know one thing I was thinking today?' said Mum, suddenly. Something in her tone indicated that the conversation was about to turn a corner.

'No, tell me,' I said.

'No, I think I'll keep it to myself.'

'No, go on. Tell me.'

'No, it's all right. It's just nothing.'

We use 'no' the way other people use 'um'. It gives greater strength to our uncertainty.

'No, it's not nothing. I can tell.'

'No, it is.'

'No, it's not.'

It was lucky the school was in a place that took some getting to.

'No, I was just thinking that I've missed out on a lot of your life, Michael.'

'Sometimes I think I've missed out on a lot of it too,' I joked.

But in spite of my efforts at a quip, I started crying. I was surprised. Even shocked, a bit like looking at yourself and realising you're bleeding. I hadn't cried since I'd sat among the bags in the cellar in Melbourne. I'd forgotten how it stung your eyes.

'Are you OK?' asked Mum when we got to the school.

'Yes.'

I went upstairs and decided I'd better give up drink. Mum went home and wrote me a letter:

Thank you for being so kind to me today and not only tonight but all through my life. You have brought joy and happiness to me and I feel very close to you. You are a very beautiful and loving person. I hated to see you shed those tears tonight. I am sorry to have upset you. Please forgive me.

There was nothing to forgive. Far from it. I was thankful that my heart was continuing to stir from its long hibernation. It was just badly hung over. Mum can track me down in my hiding places. She can make me budge emotionally. God does the same thing to me. Which is why I am careful with them both.

~

'Are you happy?' Mum will sometimes ask me, for no obvious reason except that perhaps she has noticed something in my mood before even I have.

'Yes,' I will say, doubtfully.

'I can hear a no in that yes.'

'No.'

'There's a yes in that no.'

'I wouldn't say yes if I didn't mean it,' I say, counting out the words like coins, playing them like the cards in a weak hand.

'Mean what?' says Mum.

Mum has experienced my evasive side more than most. I have spent years artfully dodging Mum's questions and evading her uncanny insights. She is so close to me that telling her important things means fronting up to them myself. Like many men, I can be quite uncommunicative when the conversation gets close to the bone. Just pretend it's not happening. The problem with being uncommunicative is that, by definition, you don't want to say too much about it. I used to worry it had something to do with being a priest but I think it's a bloke problem. Secrecy is one of the ways we make our own space within possessive relationships. Unlike God who says a lot without talking much, blokes can talk a lot without saying much.

Once, I was sitting beside my niece, then aged six, at

Christmas dinner. She had just finished her first year at school. I turned to her.

'Do you know what I do, Lara?'

'Yes. You're a priest.'

'Do you know what a priest does?'

She thought for a moment. It was a difficult question. I would have had trouble answering it myself.

'Yes,' she said. 'A priest is somebody who talks a lot.'

It starts raining. A sudden Sydney downpour. We jump back into the truck. The windscreen wiper doesn't work. The steering is dangerous in the wet. So we have to wait before we can go. Dad puts on the radio to get the scratchings for today's races. But he doesn't really listen. He takes a pill. He starts whistling. He pulls his hankie out of his pocket, balls it and throws it from palm to palm, whistling. He clicks his fingers and claps his hands over the hankie and it disappears from view for a moment. He does this when he is happy. It's a routine. We kids turn the radio over to Sammy Sparrow on 2UE. Dad doesn't mind. We ask him where the voices come from. He says there are people, smaller than ants, in the red plastic bead on top of the aerial on the bonnet. We look. We say we can see them moving around. The rain makes it difficult, but we can see them.

Eight

HAVING GOT MY OWN way in London, I also per-
suaded Mum that we should take in a few of the literary
landmarks of Britain. She's a good sport. She acquiesced.
So we headed west for Bath, the city which Jane Austen
got such a kick out of.

On the way, we paused at Windsor to look at the
castle. For the week we'd been in London, Mum had
been simmering with resentment against the monarchy. I
was amazed. She is one of the generation of Australians
for whom the arrival of the young Queen on our shores
in 1954 was the crowning moment in their sense of
nationhood. Mum described her pregnancies as they
related to those of the Queen: she was expecting my
older brother at the time Her Madge was expecting
Andrew, and so on. We watched the Sydney Opera
House go up, like a yacht unfurling its sails on the shores
of Sydney Harbour in ultra slow-motion. But for Mum,
the Opera House was significant for two reasons. The
first was that it was being built with ticket sales from the
Opera House lottery, which she hoped to win so she
could extend the house again. The second was that the

Queen was coming out to open it. Like many people, Mum became fascinated with the details of the architecture when she realised how many steps the Queen would have to climb. Mum is the same age as the Queen; at that time she stood on her feet most days of her life in a cold pharmacy until her legs ached. She felt more for the queer-old-dean. I can't explain it.

In London, however, Mum was scandalised by all the ostentatious wealth and trappings of the monarchy.

'And she doesn't even pay tax,' she said suspiciously.

Dozens of times Mum asked rhetorically who these people thought they were. She wasn't commenting on the endless royal identity crises which keep the publishing industry afloat. Floating in a gutter but afloat none the less. Mum lectured me that we come into the world with nothing and we leave it with nothing, so what was the point of all the carry-on. 'Carry-on' is one of Mum's pet expressions.

'You can't take it with you, that's the thing about it.'

'Wait till we get to Rome,' I warned.

Mum planned to go to our local tip and retrieve all the trashy magazines she'd ever bought so she could throw them out again. Her rancour came to a head at Windsor Castle. She refused to pay to get in to see the Queen's weekender until the Queen paid to come and see her in Sydney. So we went to Burger King, where they were giving away cardboard crowns with every 5000 calories. We got two and put them on our heads in the front of the Vauxhall as we made our own royal progress towards Bath.

'The Queen got her crown for free, so why shouldn't I do the same?'

Nine

IF BEING IN THE FRONT of the car with Mum for so long made me nervous, the prospect of our sharing a room was even worse. At Trixie's place, we had slept in different parts of the house. Admittedly, we had already slept side by side in the car during rests while travelling. But a shared room is a close encounter.

We found our bed-and-breakfast in Bath and made the acquaintance of the proprietor. His name was straight out of Jane Austen: Eliot. He didn't say if this was his first name or surname (possibly it was both), but launched immediately into precise instructions not just on where to park the car but how to park it. Not just how to park it, but how, in a little car like that, I should be easing my foot off the clutch. Plus a full account of how he came to feed his entire garden with tomato food and what wonderful results this had brought about. Plus various other explanations about the hardships of his life and the need for us to be careful with keys.

Eliot gave us a choice of rooms.

'But I'd recommend the one on the first floor rather than the second.'

He numbered his reasons. First, he didn't want the steps to be too much for us, especially with so much luggage. Second, he didn't think we'd like the shower which had been installed like a phone booth right in the middle of the room upstairs.

'It's more for honeymooners, that one.' He added, however, that if you ran the water at a tepid temperature, which incidentally saved him money, you wouldn't fog up the screen – honeymooners could enjoy unrivalled views over the valley while soaping up.

This was no time to start explaining that, after a delay of almost forty years, Mum *was* on her honeymoon. Sharing was going to be complex enough as far as I was concerned without leaving any margin for that kind of ambiguity.

'People what waste hot water have got themselves to blame for what views they miss out on,' Eliot went on.

'Do people really come on honeymoon to watch each other shower?'

I couldn't imagine Dad relishing the opportunity.

'Some of them do that. Some of them come to park on my front lawn,' he continued romantically. 'Some of them help themselves to my tomatoes. And some of them come to lose my keys.'

I assured him that the outlook from the upstairs shower was well worth the extra price of an '*en suite*', but that we might not have found the view inside the bedroom so restful. We may have ended up wasting hot water to preserve our modesty.

'Right. I see what you mean, then,' warming to my sense of thrift. 'I'll show you the communal bathroom.'

Eliot went away, at last, to mull over the sorry

condition of the human race and we were left to our own devices. I lugged the bags upstairs and Mum began digging deep into hers. Eventually she pulled out four telescopic coat-hangers. They were compact, designed for travelling. But they were old. I'd never seen anything like them before.

'What have you got there?' I asked.

'Have you got anything for the wash?'

'What are those hangers you've got?'

'Give me your undies and I'll wash them by hand.'

'I'm sure I can look after them myself, Mum.'

'Give them to me.'

You don't argue with Mum when she is gathering stuff for the wash. She did the laundry and hung our stuff out to dry in the room on the hangers. I mentioned that there were hangers in the rooms and the ones she brought were superfluous.

'Your father gave me these.'

'When?'

'They were inside the suitcase he gave me for our honeymoon. The one we had to throw out because of the mildew. They were meant for hanging stuff when you travel.'

~

We went up to the local pub and hoed into steak and kidney pud. The pub had declared itself a football-free zone, which meant that we were to be spared the endless intrusions of the Euro 96 competition which was on at the time. Afterwards, we strolled down the hill with a bread roll and the remains of a bottle of Australian red. With these we celebrated Mass on a modest scale, sitting under drying laundry, using the little table between our two beds for the purpose.

It's not so easy to talk about Mass, sometimes known as the Eucharist, sometimes as Communion. I imagine it's like trying to explain to someone who doesn't know your partner why you fell in love. In the years after I returned from my pilgrimage across Australia, I started sharing in a weekly Mass around the kitchen table at a community of homeless alcoholics called 'The Way'. The Way is in the inner suburbs of Melbourne; I ended up living there for a year in 1987. This was an invigorating experience of community, if a little exhausting. One of the advantages was that when the arse fell out of Wall Street in October that year it was hard for me to see what all the fuss was about. These men had the arse out of their pants the whole time.

Fourteen years later, that weekly Eucharist is still the heart of my experience of what Mass is all about, even if I don't get to The Way these days as often as I'd like. It's a pity that the only experience many people have of Mass is rarefied, ethereal, disengaged. Mass is physical. It takes place when a group, however small, draws in close to the real presence of God. Jesus lived close to the edge, both socially and emotionally, and died rough. He chose the company of rough people but related to them in the most delicate way imaginable.

At The Way, Mass took place with an old kerosene heater spluttering in the corner. People would come in gradually from the streets. Somebody would always have been in a fight and would be patched up as proceedings got under way. People interjected without inhibition: a joke, a prayer, a demand for a smoke, even a prayer for a smoke. When you look up from a table and see a small group of torn and ravaged faces, it's not so hard to recognise the face of God in the bread and wine as well.

~

Two experiences of actually being the priest at Mass stand out for me. Both had a congregation of one. The first happened about six months after I became a priest.

I was living at the time in an inner city parish where a vast bluestone church had been built in the 1870s, when the area was a shanty town settled by people who had failed on the gold fields and returned to the city very much down on their luck. There isn't much of the housing built in Richmond in the 1870s still standing, but what there is amply proves that this was a pretty poor area. It's a mystery that those people scraped together the resources to build what remains the biggest parish church in Australia. It is bigger than most of the cathedrals. It was paid for with pennies, not pounds.

In my first months as a priest, 1994, we were visited with all sorts of unnerving statements from the Vatican. One utterly excluded women from being ordained and, in spite of it being one of the most hotly debated topics among Catholics, forbade any further discussion of the matter. Another excluded divorced and remarried Catholics from Communion. Yet another insisted that the teachings of the church, known as the *Catechism*, be published in English using only gender exclusive language. It felt like somebody was filling your rucksack with bricks just for the pleasure of seeing you sweat under the load. During May in particular, the church became deeply divided in response to the Pope's categorical statement about only having male priests. In point of fact, by this time we were down to male priests who were not allergic to wheat and did not suffer from alcoholism, as we'd also had a statement excluding the use of substitutes for bread and wine at Mass. There was no knowing what would happen next. It was possible that ordination would be reserved to those, like myself, who slept poorly, on the grounds that the apostles were unable to stay awake after the last supper.

By the end of May I knew that if I had been going to be ordained that year instead of the one before, I would not have gone ahead with it. I felt that the goal posts had been moved. I was disturbed when I realised the extent to which church officials who were unable personally to reconcile the latest barrage of Vatican teaching to the New Testament, spoke out publicly in defence of the Vatican's position. I felt for them because they were living in a climate of fear. I was afraid myself.

The depression which, in the years since Peter and I made our pilgrimage, had merely lapped around my ankles from time to time was suddenly up under my throat. I was waiting to drown. In the five years after I was ordained, I gained fifteen kilos. Something was eating me.

That year, I said the 7 a.m. Mass at Richmond every Monday morning. On the Queen's birthday holiday, the first Monday in June, it was still dark at 7 a.m. and the whole world was asleep. The regulars for early Mass were understandably having the day off. I decided to go down to the church in my dressing gown and if nobody else turned up I would go back to bed myself without even opening up.

Right on seven, however, I heard footsteps on the paving. Felice had arrived. Felice was more than just the local church mouse. She was a small woman but a good talker, had grown up with 'the sisters' in a vast orphanage about two miles away, lived her whole life in the area doggedly supporting her football team and now was a kind of good Samaritan in the flats where she lived. She brought in everybody's garbage bin and did a number of other thankless chores. In a sense, she was a surviving link to a much older Richmond. It was just a nuisance to me that she'd turned up today.

As I was setting up the things for Mass, I asked Felice if there was anything she wanted to pray for in particular. She said she had come over to the church because she had heard about a terrible accident on the news the night before. Some kids were throwing stones off a freeway overpass not far away when one went through the windscreen of a Volvo and killed the young doctor who was driving. He'd only been recently married. Felice wanted to pray for his widow.

Listening to Felice, I was struck by the pettiness of my own preoccupations. The Mass I was going to celebrate took on a different hue because one of the participants, and it certainly wasn't me, had a hospitable heart. My attitude to the whole occasion thawed.

Then another curious thing happened. While I was putting everything out on the altar to get ready, Felice stood a couple of feet away on the other side chatting.

'OK, Felice, we might begin now.'

With that, she turned around and went and sat right down the back. In the very last seat. There were two of us in the church for Mass, and there were forty metres

from her to me. The space in between was cavernously
dark. It was more than just quiet, it was sepulchral. Yet,
once Mass started, the first light of dawn kissed the huge
stained-glass window in the eastern wall and ignited the
glass. Felice's face became more distinct in the gloom. I
now understand why golfers describe the experience of
being the first on the course in the early light of day,
when the dew is undisturbed and every footprint on it is
the first, as mystical. The air in the church was still.
Writers know the effect a blank piece of paper can
produce: it can stir a sense of fear, awe, possibility,
adventure, even hunger. A vacant church can do this too.
People who complain that churches aren't full forget
that they are also made to be empty.

Felice and I were standing on either side of a kind of
abyss. Yet we were both human beings with hungers and
needs. Mass can only be celebrated by human beings. At
the same time, if you take God seriously, it can only
be celebrated on the edge of a precipice. You can't look
into a cup of wine, repeat Jesus' words, 'This is my
blood', and think that you're at some kind of a feel-good
workshop.

~

Mum and I had Mass in a little room in a bed-and-
breakfast in Bath, the first of many such experiences
along the way. There is a gulf between us. There have
been many gaps in our understanding. But at least we
could share our own speechlessness that God who is so
inscrutable should be so close. Our knees were almost
touching. All three of us.

I was soon wondering why I had been so anxious

about sharing the room with Mum. I'm the one who snores, after all, a problem she had obviously thought about in advance and dealt with by making sure she was at least the first asleep. We got ready for bed. Mum looked out the window and noticed Eliot in the distant end of the garden. She said that the garden reminded her of the one her father created at their home in Mowbray Road. Her father used to do the garden long into the dusk, forever putting off the moment when he had to come inside the house. It had almost slipped my mind that Mum was now, for the first time, in the country of her father, John Baxter, the man we heard so much less about than our famous grandfather, Greg McGirr.

I had been worrying about Mum repossessing me and forgetting that she had a life of her own. It's quite liberating to find your mother has things on her mind other than you. At least, it's liberating for the half hour before you start resenting the fact that you are not her total obsession.

Dad is coming back to the car. Mum's car. He has been speaking with the priest. Father Dynon asks him if we can have a home-Mass at our end of the parish, if he can say Mass in our house and invite the neighbours. Dad tells him that he can say Mass in our house as long as Dad can sleep in the priest's church.

Ten

I SUPPOSE SOME PEOPLE go to Bath in the belief that
a bath is such a rare find in Britain that a town is named
after one. Bath is, in fact, a bizarre Georgian fantasy built
around the remains of a Roman spa. In the abbey, there
is a monument to one of the local boys who made good,
Captain Arthur Phillip. Phillip was the first governor of
New South Wales, as much in the sense that a prison has
a governor as a colony does. If you take in what the eighteenth century did to Bath, and appreciate the tiredness
of culture that makes a fetish of the past, the exhaustion
that haphazardly loots history for some sense of style
which can be turned to a quick buck, you realise that
some of the trendiest ideas of the late twentieth century
have had an earlier vogue. You also think that Botany
Bay must have been a long way from the delicate social
fabric of Bath which Jane Austen describes in *Persuasion*.

We didn't visit Jane Austen's Bath. It doesn't exist
anymore. In *Persuasion*, a character called Lady Russell
gets vexed by her 'intercourse in Camden Place'.
Camden Place is still there but the usage of the word
'intercourse' has shrunk. We had a teacher at school

who told us that in the world of *Pride and Prejudice*, large families were accustomed to 'use their balls for intercourse'. After thirty years in the classroom, most of them in the same oily dark green suit, he still did not understand why teenage boys found the comment distracting. This is testimony to the breadth of his mind, not its narrowness. In *Persuasion*, Lady Russell explains that she gets vexed in the way that 'a person in Bath who drinks the water, gets all the new publications, and has a very large acquaintance, has time to be vexed'.

We drank the water in Bath, tried to get some new publications and only made one acquaintance, Eliot. And he wasn't even very large. In search of the new publications, we found our way into the smallest book shop to press for business this side of Gutenberg. Notwithstanding its size, the shop assistant said the place had five owners. Each of them had their own special interest as a collector. Sure enough, crammed into the little shop, were five bookcases. They were labelled, *Gypsies, Hunting, Erotica, Travel* and *Dogs*. I asked after a couple of titles.

'Oh, you want books for reading,' said the assistant, sounding surprised.

We drank the water at no less a venue than the Georgian pump room and were congratulated by the waitress as being among the few patrons who ever finished a glass. It was vile but we'd paid 45 *p* and weren't going to be deterred by such a small consideration as taste. The menu told us that, in Jane Austen's time, these waters were prescribed by the gallon and visitors often complained about a lack of toilet facilities. We had already found our toilets, in McDonald's of course. I think every McDonald's in the world has toilets upstairs and at the back. Gents on your left. I zipped up my fly and turned around just in time to notice large wads of money being passed from one cubicle to another. Fifty yards from the pump room, on a Saturday morning, drugs were being sold. Jane Austen doesn't say much about that.

In the pump room, Mum talked about the boss she had during the war, Mr Rose. I didn't know much about him. Every day, he went out and had a Sargent's Meat Pie and came back to the chemist shop suffering such severe indigestion that he immediately had to have two tablespoons of bicarb of soda. But that never stopped him going out the following day and doing exactly the same thing all over. Perhaps he felt slightly guilty about his little weakness, because he regularly returned to the shop with some Bath Buns for his apprentices.

'But these,' Mum assures me looking up from the Bath Buns which have now arrived, 'these are the real thing.' I should have hoped so, although I've heard that the fried chicken in Kentucky is not necessarily the world's best.

~

Mum's life as an apprentice was far from easy. At the age of sixteen, she was having lectures in the morning at Sydney University then hot-footing it down to be in the shop by 1 p.m., grabbing lunch on the way. She also worked Saturday mornings and evenings.

When I was ordained, Mum took me to see *The Phantom of the Opera* at the new Theatre Royal in Sydney. The highlight of the evening for me was Mum's casual comment, looking across the street, 'That's where I used to work.' Sure enough, among all the new chrome and cement, a couple of buildings in King Street had managed to survive. One, on the corner, was a hotel which was now operating as a bank. Wrapped around it was a strange-shaped building still called Culwalla Chambers and, on the King Street side on the ground floor, the place where Mum cut her teeth as a young chemist, grinding powders and blending ointments. Rose's Pharmacy. Mum could close her eyes and visualise a different King Street. There used to be a furrier's next door to the chemist and a corsetry shop around the corner; a door led to a narrow staircase where people went upstairs to buy sheet music. Opposite were a jeweller's, Repins Cafe and the old Theatre Royal.

As a young woman, Mum had to compete for her career with all the returned soldiers. They were given preference for places in courses at uni. She was standing in Rose's on the day victory in the Pacific was declared. She remembers it vividly. People danced in the streets and rode on the top of trams. Mr Rose had to close the shop for the rest of the day for fear that so much merriment might end in vandalism. The following day it was back to the grindstone, even if some people had a sore head. In the years after the war, when Bradman made a comeback from the injuries which for him had luckily coincided with the war years, Mum used to go around the corner at lunch time to listen to the cricket on the radio in the sports store which Stan McCabe had retired into.

Mum remembers her future mother-in-law buying sheet music upstairs and her future father-in-law coming into the shop. Greg McGirr senior had been a cabinet minister, had staged several dramatic fights with Premier Jack Lang, and knew everybody in Sydney. It might be more accurate to say that he liked to be known by everyone in Sydney. Greg McGirr was himself a pharmacist by trade and the acquaintance with Rose was probably long-standing. Greg was not a small man. There are more photos of him than anybody in the whole clan; more photos even than of the famous Jack Lang. One of the first things you notice in my aunt's place in London is a portrait of him taken by Fredrich, the Annie Leibovitz of his day, at the Waldorf Hotel in New York in 1939. In those days, portrait photographers worked like snipers and each had a post from which he could shoot bystanders. It was a chancy enterprise in which opportunity counted for almost as much as skill. Fredrich's post at the Waldorf was a measure of his status but, after the war, even the streets of Sydney were sprinkled with photographers.

According to Trixie, Greg McGirr kept most of them in business. He never refused to buy a print of himself. There must have been a photographer based more or less permanently outside Repins Cafe in King Street, opposite Rose's Pharmacy. Repins was not quite Sydney's Waldorf but it was the haunt of the first generation of Australians able to spell the word 'cappuccino'. Along with Lorenzini's, it has been immortalised in Les Murray's poem 'An Absolutely Ordinary Rainbow'.

There are photos of Greg McGirr with his wife, Rachel Miller, and many of his children, taken at different times on this very spot. Often, on birthdays, he took his children across the street to Mr Rose. Mum can't remember either Dad or Trixie coming into the shop, they were probably too old for this by the time Mum was working, but she certainly remembers my youngest aunt, Nona, being proudly introduced to Mr Rose as 'the birthday girl'. Mum was out the back counting pills.

The shop is now a travel agent. It is doubtless one of the many places from which Mum has brought home literature at one time or another.

~

Mum started in pharmacy before penicillin was on the market and was still working when Viagra became the latest wonder. She was astonished at the age of her first Viagra customer, a returned soldier, old enough to have been her first penicillin customer as well. As an active Catholic, she found herself working in a difficult business when the Church announced its ban on artificial contraception in the late sixties. Priests sometimes talk about the amount of work they did at that time helping Catholics negotiate this unnecessary obstacle. I'm sure they did. But they overlook the huge amount of agonised moral discussion in which sympathetic doctors and pharmacists took part and for which they were equipped with only common sense.

A theologian did tell me once, somewhat ambiguously, that Paul VI, who announced the ban, never caused a pharmacy to close its doors. Actually the theologian was wrong, because Mum took the day off work in 1970 when Paul VI visited Australia.

She took us to Randwick Racecourse to wait for hours until the Pope came to say Mass. There were more than two people present that day. Dad was with us. He was far more familiar with the racecourse than Mum and got us seats in the stand right on the finishing post. These were the best seats on race day but unfortunately the Pope hadn't come for the races. We didn't have much of a view of the makeshift altar which was miles in the distance.

Dad folded his Mass booklet down the middle and put it in his pocket like a race book. We knelt reverently during parts of the Mass.

'I bet you've never knelt here before,' Mum said to Dad. Mum had made the mistake of saying 'I bet'. Dad couldn't resist.

'I've said plenty of prayers in this place, believe you me, pet.'

'But I bet you haven't been down on your knees.'

'Only when I've dropped my betting slip, pet.'

For twenty-five years, Mum has spent most of her working life standing in a dispensary in a busy chemist shop at Ermington, one of the countless western suburbs of Sydney. The area used to be largely public housing, but, like most public assets, the properties have been gradually sold off. Mum works in a shop where two or three pharmacists work cheek by jowl in an area about the size of a fast-food van. The premises are in Betty Cuthbert Avenue, named after the most famous *émigré* from the area, an Olympic runner who won three gold medals in Melbourne in 1956 and another in Tokyo in 1964. She shared with Mum the fact that her plans to get to Rome between those two fixtures went haywire.

We come from a heavily medicated part of the world. People put their faith in drugs, pills, coloured capsules, powders, patches, tablets and tabsules. Stories are confided to Mum across the pharmacy counter under the pretext of health care. I don't know if it's the pills that make the difference or just seeing the familiar face of someone willing to take a bit of an interest. Someone who knows your name. Mum will say it's been a busy day when she hasn't been able to make a cup of coffee. It's been a quieter day when she's made a cup of coffee in the morning, put it down beside the computer and tipped it out, untouched and stone cold, before she knocks off at six o'clock.

In all those years, I've only heard a small number of stories about Mum's life at work. It's a daily grind. With very little magic. Ermington is a typical lower-middle-class Australian suburb. It has the ability to impose anonymity on every kind of human problem and, for that matter, every kind of achievement.

A couple of years ago, I was among a handful of mourners gathered on a wet Friday morning in January in an unprepossessing red brick church a few doors from Mum's pharmacy. I had read about a funeral in the paper and was curious. The day before, another Pope had beatified Mary MacKillop at Randwick Racecourse. Two hundred thousand people had been there give or take. Only a couple of dozen attended the service for Thomas Mayne, who had died quietly at the age of ninety-four. He was a chemical engineer. Sixty years previously, he'd invented Milo. The project took four years but the final product currently earns Nestle $550 million every year in thirty countries. Mayne didn't get a share: he was a company man. Mourners heard that he put his loyalty to Nestle above everything else, even, at times, his family. It was marvellous, in his case, the difference Milo didn't make.

~

There are many advantages in being a pharmacist. One is that, after a lifetime deciphering the scrawl that doctors put on prescriptions, Mum can read any handwriting on earth. Under any circumstances. When we visited the galleries of the British Library, we discovered that they had on display letters, diaries and manuscripts in the handwriting of such notables as Johnson, Boswell, Dryden, Dickens and Wordsworth. I am ashamed to report that the handwriting of some of our greatest literary figures isn't all that you'd hope for. I found them impossible to decipher. Mum on the other hand began effortlessly reciting Wordsworth back to me. And then Dryden. I could hardly believe that these gentlemen had an audience of pharmacists in mind.

'OK, Mum. We can get these books out of the library and read them later.'

Eleven

IN BATH, WE BEGAN to notice the amount of time travellers spend writing home. Whenever we sat down for a cup of what passes for coffee in England, there'd be somebody at the next table twisting clichés – 'Weather here, wish you were perfect' – on the backs of postcards. Occasionally, somebody appeared to be writing something more interesting, so we'd manoeuvre ourselves until Mum could read the appalling handwriting.

Postcards do nasty things to people. A couple of weeks later, Mum and I queued for an hour to get into the Louvre in Paris. People waiting with us suggested that the Louvre should be run like Disneyland and have individual queues for each 'big' painting. Once inside, we heard the familiar sound of thongs flopping on the marble floor behind us. We looked around and saw a fellow Australian, bringing credit to his country by getting around the Louvre in a graceless pair of shorts and a T-shirt which had long given up any hope of ever meeting his navel again.

'Mona Lisa?' he yelled loudly. Our travels through Siena and Florence had made us curious about

Leonardo, so we were also interested in smiling back at dear Lisa. An attendant pointed him through the next door and we followed, but he out-paced us and we heard the balletic sound of thongs flopping into the distance. Later, however, we found him again. He'd got lost.

'Mona Lisa, Mona Lisa?' he demanded of another attendant. At least he didn't try to sing it.

'If I were that guide, I'd point him in the wrong direction, just to give him some exercise,' said Mum.

This is evidently what happened, as we found him again between Holbein and Dürer.

'Mona Lisa?' he yelled. 'I just want to see the bloody *Mona Lisa*. I've paid top dollar to get into this joint and I want to see the damned bitch.'

'Surely, he should say top franc,' said Mum.

The sign of a great gallery is that visitors will spend more time in the postcard shop than they will looking at the paintings. I suppose that a postcard, being something you can actually buy and own, will always exercise a stronger fascination than something you have to leave behind when you go. The card shop at the Louvre is enormous. There would be plenty of room in it to hang some paintings where people are likely to notice them.

We ran into our fellow Australian again in the card shop. He had picked up dozens of postcards of the *Mona Lisa*. When he got to the counter he asked for still more of them, which had to be got out of stock. He was obviously going to catch up on a hefty amount of correspondence.

'So you found it?' I asked as we both stood at the counter.

'Found what?'

'The *Mona Lisa*. What did you think of it?'

'I can tell you one thing, mate. She's nothing to write home about.'

~

In Bath, we made a point of visiting the source and origin of all postcards, the home of all post. The world's first pre-paid postage stamp, the so-called penny black, was franked there in 1840. Bath achieved this distinction because of the incompetence of the postmaster who failed to follow instructions and franked the stamps a day ahead of everybody else. I'm sure some big shots in London were cheesed off. The shop in Bath which ushered in a new era of communication is now a museum, staffed by moth-eaten volunteers. It's hard to imagine that 150 years ago, ready access to an effective mail network was as significant as the Internet.

Leaving Bath, we tried to pick up the trail of some of my life-long heroines and heroes. Ironically, some of these were people whose lives, in the years after 1840, came to depend on the post. In Yorkshire we wanted to go to Haworth and pay homage at the Brontë parsonage. In Birmingham we aimed for a place known as 'The Oratory', in which Cardinal John Henry Newman had lived for many years, before he died there, as an old man, in 1891. Newman and the Brontës were both great for the mail business.

In the middle of the nineteenth century, Newman was clearly the more widely known. He was a national figure in the revival of Anglicanism in the 1830s and a prominent convert to Roman Catholicism in 1845. In the

1840s, the years in which *Wuthering Heights* and *Jane Eyre* were written, the Brontës lived a monastic kind of existence at Haworth. In her account of the life of Charlotte Brontë, Elizabeth Gaskell writes as a friend. She has one line that speaks volumes. *Her life at Haworth was so unvaried that the postman's call was the event of her day.* I know what that means. I have lived in religious communities where people wait breathlessly for the mail or the phone to ring. It's a sign of isolation.

John Henry Newman wrote enough letters in his lifetime to cover the back of every postcard on sale at the Louvre. This is a little odd, because Newman was something of a luddite. He resisted even such a new-fangled contrivance as the fountain pen because he didn't like the feel of steel in his hand. But he licked a lot of stamps. Even so, Newman is not remembered simply as a reliable correspondent.

Newman reshaped the sub-culture I am part of. So many of the ideas which have breathed new life into Catholicism in the twentieth century and which were taken on board at Vatican II, our high-water mark, were pioneered by Newman in the nineteenth century. Among these is the idea that Christian teaching is not rigid like a building but grows like a tree. He also articulated the view that the ultimate teaching authority in the church is the conscience of the individual Christian which, somewhat cannily, he labelled the *aboriginal vicar of Christ*. The Pope is sometimes known as 'the vicar of Christ'.

Imagine that Christianity in the English-speaking world of the nineteenth century was on the verge of a massive heart attack, its veins and arteries clogged by generations of fast fatty food. Newman invented by-pass surgery. He gave us a new lease on life. It's as dramatic as that.

~

Strangely enough, I admire in the Brontës exactly what I admire in Newman. The imagination fighting free. Anyone who's read *Jane Eyre* or *Wuthering Heights* will recognise the sheer force with which the prose breaks out of boxes. Gaskell says of Charlotte, *she must not hide her gift in a napkin.* Consider what 1847–48 was like for Charlotte Brontë. Her brother, Branwell, died from consumption in September, aged thirty-one; Emily, her sister, got the bug at his funeral and died at Christmas, aged thirty; Anne, her other sister, joined them the following May, aged twenty-nine. Charlotte received a negative review of *Jane Eyre* in the post within a couple of weeks of burying her sister Emily. Gaskell writes feelingly, *she was numbed to all petty annoyances by the grand severity of Death.*

Death is spelt with a capital D. It was a character in their lives; it was a family member in every house in Haworth. As the village turned from agriculture to light industry, the population of Haworth grew last century out of all proportion to the ability of sewerage and water systems to cope. By the 1850s, the average life expectancy was twenty-five; the infant mortality rate was forty-one per cent. Charlotte once told Gaskell that she knew *her death would be quite lonely.* Gaskell said that Charlotte *works off a great deal that is morbid* into *her writing and* out *of her life.*

On a warm summer's afternoon, the narrow winding streets of Haworth seem anything but death traps. They throb with life. Mum and I walked slowly from the railway station up to the parsonage, a bit of a haul. Only when we got to the top did we discover that the land on one side of the parsonage has been given over to an enormous car park, so we could have saved ourselves the effort. On the other hand, *Wuthering Heights* loses something if you try to imagine Heathcliff and Cathy running towards each other across a crowded car park, especially if their plaintive voices are lost in the gutturals of buses warming up, hinting to their passengers that it's time to move on.

This was once a lonely place; now you queue to get in and follow a carefully mapped route through the house, which prevents congestion by making sure that nobody redoubles their steps. Finally, as always, you make it to the souvenir shop. Here you can buy copies of any of the main Brontë books for a quid, the cost of two postcards. But the postcards sell a lot better. You can also buy videos: the staff work all day every day with Larry Olivier's film version of *Wuthering Heights* running continually in the background. A complete screening will fit comfortably more than fifteen times into any working week. I hope someone is getting a stress loading.

In spite of this, the parsonage stops you short. Inside the front door is Mr Brontë's study. He took his meals on his own in here and could only read the psalms with the aid of a magnifying glass. On the other side of a narrow corridor, his three daughters circled their working table until late in the night, reading to each other what they had written. Brontë, the parson, provokes indignation.

Any man who, in spite of his blindness, takes a loaded pistol to bed every night and discharges the bullet out his window the following morning makes me nervous.

Thousands visit the parsonage but only a fraction of them seem to make it over to the church where blind Mr Brontë, unable to look at any clock, preached every week for precisely half an hour. He knew when to stop. (I'm lucky to get away with five minutes.) I looked around the church as if it, too, were an extension of the museum, until I found a simple 'prayer tree' at the back. Here people write down the names of those who need help: the sick, the sad and the sour. They are entrusted to the prayers of a community which is invisible among so many day visitors but evidently still alive. I noticed some girls reading the prayer tree. They had annoyed me in the museum because they kept asking if they could try on all the Brontës' dresses then giggling when they were told they couldn't. The dresses were, admittedly, the right size for them. A recent biographer argues that Emily Brontë had anorexia nervosa. Once the girls had left the church, I went over to the prayer tree because I'd assumed they were going to vandalise it. They hadn't. They had written down the name of a thirteen-year-old friend back home who was waiting anxiously for a bone marrow transplant.

Something similar happened in Stratford-on-Avon. When we went to look for his tomb, we realised that Shakespeare had actually retired from the theatre and spent some years as a lay minister in the parish close to where he grew up. If the thought of Shakespeare as a young lad sitting in a classroom is enough to threaten any teacher worth their salt, imagine coming to church and hearing Shakespeare read from a Bible in the language to which he added so much colour, subtlety and flexibility. The Bible he used is still on the stand. But at the back of Shakespeare's church are the rather gauche creations of 'the Sunday club'. One of them asks you if you can 'find the lost sheep': you look under little paper flaps and see first a cat, then a mouse and finally the sheep. In the ubiquitous souvenir shop, selling the ubiquitous pencil sharpeners and erasers – everything, in other words, that you need to write on the ubiquitous postcards – a volunteer attendant is telling the woman behind the counter that somebody from the area has just been taken to hospital. He says over and over that 'it sounds serious'. There is hardly the subtlety of Shakespeare in that sibilance, but except for the fact that folk with clumsy tongues in small communities express concern for each other how best they can, there would never have been any such thing as Shakespeare. He would have had nothing to write about and nobody to understand him.

'They wouldn't have mentioned it if it weren't serious,' says the attendant, this time over the heads of an excursion of school kids.

As we were leaving the church in Haworth, a middle-aged woman appeared with her elderly mother on her arm. The mother was blind.

'This must be Catholic,' said the old woman loudly. 'It smells Catholic. Don't you think it smells Catholic?'

The entire graveyard outside turned in one movement.

'It doesn't smell *that* good,' said Mum.

~

Since John Henry Newman died, 14 000 people have signed the visitors' book in his rooms. The Brontë Parsonage probably gets that many visitors every week during the high season but Newman's rooms are not really open to the public.

I spent years identifying Newman with a bundle of bright ideas. It was only by chance that Newman emerged for me as flesh and blood. The reason was a small, brown leather suitcase with a failing leather handle.

In 1995, I was working on a magazine which decided to publish something for the sesquicentenary of Newman's conversion. We wanted to do this to remind the readers, who happened to include my mother, how much less antagonistic Anglicans and Catholics had become towards each other. I noticed on the last page of a biography of Newman (I had skipped to there from about page 150) that just before he died, a niece turned up from Australia to visit him. This was Grace Langford, the only child of Newman's sister Harriet. So I sent off a fax to the Oratory asking if perhaps they knew of any Australian relatives of the Cardinal. I thought this might add a bit of colour. They told me that Grace had a son, Frank, whose granddaughter they believed was living in Melbourne. They gave me her surname and I started working through the Melbourne phone directory.

'That's not me,' said a male voice, after half a dozen calls.

'I'm sorry to have disturbed you then.'

I was hanging up.

'That's my wife.'

Harriet's great-great-granddaughter was living in a

single-bedroom downstairs flat in a block that didn't get much sunlight. She and her husband were more interested in showing me their four-wheel-drive than in talking about last century's cardinals. They were about to set off on a four months tour of the outback, complete with long-range phones and car fridges. They'd get plenty of sunlight there. But finally we went inside.

'We killed him, you know.'

'What do you mean?'

'The Cardinal caught the bug that killed him from Grace.'

The story about Newman catching his last cold from his Australian niece had survived in the family by word of mouth for five generations. Other than that, however, they didn't have a lot to say. I was shown a copy of the same biography that I had given up on myself: their bookmark had not made it much further into the undergrowth than mine. Slightly disappointed, I finished my cup of tea and made ready to leave.

'But we've got some letters. We've got some letters the Cardinal wrote. I'm not sure if you'd want to see them.'

I was sure that I would. They produced a small leather suitcase, inside a black pillowslip. In the case were about a dozen letters that Newman had written to his Australian connections. There were also a number of letters from his eccentric brother Frank. And, in a number of small red volumes, Harriet's entire diaries over a period of twenty years or more.

This material didn't re-route the entire course of Newman scholarship. But what emerged from that small case were vibrant personalities. It was like rubbing the lantern and conjuring a real presence.

Newman had been close to Harriet. Inside the suitcase was a tiny envelope and inside the envelope, in two small squares of paper, was a tender poem he had composed for her in 1830:

> *Loved wherever known!*
> *Sure this is a blessing*
> *That's worth the false tone*
> *Of a proud world's confessing.*

In addition, there is a longer letter to Harriet's husband, Tom Mozley, recounting the beginnings of the Oxford Movement, which Newman says he has been *detailing in various letters till I am quite sick of it*:

> *We want (1) to stir up the clergy to reflection (2) to maintain the doctrine of the Apostolical Succession (3) to defend the prayer book. Many objects will follow and we will begin publishing tracts. We hope to have about 12 Oxford names ...*

One of the 'objects' which followed, sadly, was a complete break with Harriet, who suspected Newman of almost luring her husband into the Roman fold in 1843. Newman was never reconciled with the sister he loved. The small case included a letter he sent to Tom Mozley on the occasion of Harriet's death on July 18, 1852. John Henry had not seen her for nine years.

> *My dearest Mozley,*
> *You may think without my saying a word how your letter startled and shocked me. May that God*

who made you and loves you give you to the full
that consolation which you so greatly need and
which he alone can give you.
Yours affectionately.
John H Newman

Two days later, he wrote to Mozley again, this time on black-bordered paper:

Thank you for your kind notice but I shall not
avail myself of it. I shall not forget the hour.

Portraits and photos of Newman can look severe. According to Lytton Strachey, Newman's *bête noire*, Cardinal Manning, described him as 'a great hater'. His letters, on the other hand, reveal the full gamut of human experience.

One letter, in particular, leaves an indelible impression. Again it is to Mozley. The watermark on the paper is 1884. The hand is spidery. On the reverse side another hand has added 'the last', indicating that this is probably the last letter that arrived in Australia:

I ought to have reminded myself that before I
became a Catholic I hindered you from becoming
one. This leads me to say that I think my second
judgement in all respects a better than the first.
Yours affectionately, JHN.

The letter shows no regrets about his decision. But it also implies an acknowledgement of the pain the decision may have caused.

Newman's published diaries and correspondence currently occupy twenty-seven volumes. The small collection in the suitcase includes the original copy of the final letter Newman sent in his life. Dated August 2, 1890, it lets Grace know he would be delighted to see her. He has dictated it to his secretary, William Neville, but the initials are unmistakably his own. It contains an ominous message:

I am sometimes engaged with the doctors.

Alongside this is a book of poems which Newman presented to Grace. It is initialled *for G.L. from J.H.N., 1890.* The hand is feeble. The volume still contains a printed notice of Newman's requiem which Grace must have inserted almost immediately. Apparently she said afterwards that she wished she had not removed her gloves and offered him a cold hand.

~

Birmingham is an inelegant city. It's probably not as congested as London but it feels worse. Looking at Birmingham is like watching somebody trying to carry too many bags when there's nothing you can do to help. But the thickness of only one wall from Hagley Road, Edgbaston, the major artery of the city, is the sepulchral parlour of the Oratory. Here we waited for Gerard Tracey, who was to be our guide. Gerard is the archivist of the Oratory. He had been editing the final volumes of Newman correspondence and preparing his cause for canonisation. He is the kind of person you seldom meet now. His entire life's work has been as a servant of the very considerable Newman legacy. A mutual friend told me that Gerard lives in a modest council flat.

Gerard and Mum seemed to hit it off straight away. She told him how disgusted she was with all the possessions of the royal family.

'These so-called great people,' she says. 'They make themselves look great. But at the end of the day, who are they really?'

I've heard all this before but Gerard agrees readily.

'You can't take it with you,' says Mum.

You couldn't guess Gerard's age by looking at him, or even, I suspect, by measuring the fall of his long hair. He happened to be forty-one and had spent eighteen years at the Oratory. He showed us the gate through which Grace, the niece from Australia, had arrived to visit. Newman had had a fall the year before that, so he couldn't come downstairs to greet her. It was summer, so although there had been a sudden drop in temperature, there had been no fire in the room where they sat. He caught pneumonia.

'Within two days,' says Gerard emphatically, 'that was that.'

After Newman died, his secretary and literary executor, William Neville, moved into what had been his room, to handle a vast correspondence. The result was that the room was never cleaned out. It never has been. It stands today as if Newman had just gone down the street for a few minutes. The room is still inhabited by him: full of paper clutter, a leather armchair in one of the few places with much light beside the window. Gerard reminded us that the Victorian taste for dark interiors, although even contemporary visitors described the room as monastic. He pulled open the breviary Newman had acquired on the death of a dear friend, Harold Froude, and had continued to read daily for the rest of his life. Gerard returned the bookmarks to their places in case the Cardinal suddenly came through the door. He then reached for what he said was the most remarkable thing in the room: the inside cover of an exercise book, on which Newman had recorded the major changes in his heart since he was a callow evangelical youth. It is an autobiography in about a dozen sentences. 'And now a Cardinal,' reads the last entry cryptically, waiting even at that late stage for the next development. Newman never settled. He kept gingering his own soul.

The bedroom is divided neatly down the middle; on the other side of a partition is where Newman's bed once stood. When he was made a Cardinal by the progressive Leo XIII, he discovered a rule which stipulated that Cardinals should have their own private chapels. This was because they should maintain the lustre of being a prince of the church by only saying Mass in public when it could be done with a certain level of pomp. Newman complied with the letter of the law by moving into a guest room to sleep and replacing his bed with a makeshift altar behind the partition. Around it, in front of him as he knelt there, he put the photos of the people he loved, many of whom pre-deceased him. Their memorial cards are curling now. His cardinal's zucchetta and wide-brimmed red hat, together with his red ceremonial robes, are stuck unceremoniously in a shipping case behind him. Gerard explained that becoming a Cardinal meant a lot to Newman because it legitimated what he and so many of his friends had stood for and suffered for. But the trappings horrified him.

It so happened that his improvised chapel was under a boys' dormitory. Some loose tongues put it about that this was unbecoming for the man with a red hat. So while Newman was in Rome the dormitory was relocated.

The thing about Newman's room is not that it is so bizarre. On the contrary, it is completely familiar to me. It is the room of most of the Jesuits I have ever lived with. Large, high-ceilinged, down-at-heel, full of clutter, the only clear space is the bottom of the waste-paper basket because nothing can ever be thrown out. There is plenty in a room like this which is close to the heart of the inhabitant, but it isn't on display; it's tucked away somewhere. The stuff on the walls could be anyone's and will probably be left behind when he moves on. No fresh flowers, not even pot plants. The bed linen is dull, usually threadbare. There will be half a dozen dog-eared toothbrushes forgotten in the bottom of a drawer somewhere; his underwear could well be in a filing cabinet. It isn't a place for play. And not for company. It's a place you have on your own. But please God it is still a place for love.

Twelve

MUM'S LUGGAGE INCLUDED a magnificent white cosmetic case. The staff of Crown Street Women's Hospital had passed around the hat when she left to get married in 1959 and presented it to her. They all knew she was going on a big trip, so it was the obvious thing to give. Besides, most of her colleagues were already moving from the hospital into retail pharmacy, the newly expanding world of toiletries and free perfume samples, and they knew where their bread was going to be buttered. The expense for Mum of keeping the bag stocked for the rest of her life would mean that none of them need ever fear hunger.

We only ever picked up clues from Mum about her career in the dispensary at Crown Street. It was no place for the naive. The fifties were among the toughest times for working women in Australian history. In the twenties they were less custom-bound; women are prominent, for example, among our early aviators and motoring enthusiasts. During the war they ran the country – a belief my mother has reiterated many times. But when 500 000 Australians were demobbed at the end of the war, out of a population of 8 000 000, it was a case of 'roll over honey'. Equal pay for equal work, the only remotely feminist slogan I heard Mum use, was a long way off. During the fifties, Mum scraped and scrounged on sixty per cent of the male wage to save for a new car, a Morris Oxford.

At Crown Street, there was a special ward for unmarried mothers. In the time Mum was working there, the youngest new mother was only nine years old, probably an incest victim. The oldest was fifty-two. Mum was troubled by the behaviour of one of the senior staff members, who seemed to have the authority to distribute the babies of unwed mothers to the childless couples of whom she personally approved. It's hard to imagine any greater form of power. To this day, if a married friend has a child Mum refers to a 'baby'. The child of an unmarried person is an 'infant'. The more formal word does not imply any judgement on Mum's part, although she does believe that the best place to bring up children is within a marriage. The formality developed to control pain. In the fifties, relatively few unwed mothers kept their babies. You couldn't get gooey over an infant the way you could over a baby.

~

Mum walked to work from Central Station, through what were then the slums of Surry Hills. Out of the corner of her eye, she took in the lives that Ruth Park and Kylie Tennant had described in fiction. There was a time, soon after Dad got sick, when I became obsessed about money because I thought we were going broke. I'm not sure why I was so worried because I can't remember a time when Dad had a job anyway, although he did contrive a number of schemes. At one point he leased an old milkbar nearby, at the Cammeray shops, and decided to turn it into a real estate agency. Mum worked like a Trojan – another of her favourite expressions – to make the shop presentable but, before long, all that remained of the blood, sweat and tears were a wooden step-ladder we kept under the house with the honeymoon bag and a set of milkshake glasses which any collector of twentieth-century antiques would die for.

At the age of eleven, I was saving obsessively, searching for soft-drink bottles to return for the deposit and trying to find odd jobs. I converted all my change into dollar notes and piled them up, counting them over and over like a miser. Once I got into trouble for pinching money from the charity well under the boar that sits outside Sydney Hospital in Macquarie Street. When Mum asked for an explanation, I blurted out something about us being poor. Mum was taken aback.

'I'll show you what poverty is. I'll take you for a walk through Surry Hills where I used to work. Then you'll see poverty. Don't be so bloody stupid.'

Mum never took me on that walk but it was apparent that she had a broader perspective than mine.

~

Crown Street Hospital was literally a stone's throw from one of the most successful industries in post-war Australia. This was where Bex was made. Bex was part of a range of powders and tablets called APCs. Vincent's was another famous brand. The two products used saturation advertising campaigns: 'Take Vincent's with confidence' vied with 'Bex is better' as the most familiar slogan in Australia. APC stood for Aspirin, Phenacetin and Caffeine, which explains why Vincent's boasted of 'three-way pain relief'. APCs were a cross between a headache powder and a pick-me-up. You'd see people stopping at kiosks or ducking into milkbars to buy a single powder and toss it down their throats with a glass of water. These drugs were so much part of the culture of silent survival of the fifties that stress was spoken of only in terms of the need for 'a cup of tea, a Bex and a good lie down'. Overuse of APCs had some dire health consequences.

Dad used an especially strong type of APC called Pirofin. When we went away on trips, which we did seldom and always cut short because Dad became restless away from home, Mum's cosmetic case was adapted to accommodate a couple of large bottles of this stuff. Even if Mum had any idea of the long-term implications of Dad's behaviour, she was powerless in the face of compulsive behaviour. Dad liked to take his Pirofin with fresh orange juice, which Mum squeezed in an old plastic juicer. This was how Dad started the day. I think the acid in the fruit gave the pills an extra kick. During the day, he would stop at milkbars and buy a glass of the fruit punch which used to sit on the counter in a refrigerated goldfish bowl with an arm swinging through it to stop the contents settling.

Whenever Dad went out in his beloved truck, he always wore a sports jacket and an Al-Capone-style fedora. It's a pity he didn't live long enough to see his regular outfit become the height of post-punk *couture* in the eighties. We thought he looked like a nerd. Then nerds became trendy. He only wore white shirts and braces. Generally, he put on a self-tying tie. Yet in his own youth, he had gone out on a limb to wear all this – what became a very conservative wardrobe. His father used to refer dismissively to his sports jackets as 'those things which Gregory wears'.

Twenty-five years later, Dad's sports jacket was anything but casual. Before leaving the house, an ancient wallet was loaded into its inside pocket and his loose change went into the right-hand pocket. His truck had no indicators, so if Dad was making a left-hand turn he would reach into his supply of coins, roll down the window and bang on the roof with the coin. I guess the people behind got the message. Sometimes one of us had to hold the truck in gear while all this was going on. In the left-hand pocket Dad kept his supply of Pirofin.

Dad never washed a cup or saucer and never made himself a cup of tea. He was incapable of anything so practical. He was capable of being funny and tender. He loved bouncing us on his knee, a game we called 'chip-chops', and twirling us around by our arms, which we called 'aeroplane spins'. When, in 1969, he heard that his mother had died, he came and sat in front of the TV and sank deep into his favourite chair. I asked him why he wasn't crying. I said that if our mum had died, we'd be crying. He was moved by this. He gave Mum a big hug. When we were up country for some reason or other, he would tell us about country towns he'd stayed in when he was single and what he'd done.

'I never thought I'd come back here with a lovely wife and three lovely children.' He said it often. He meant it. He couldn't believe his luck. He had known what it was like to be lonely. We loved him.

But Dad was in the grip of forces that none of us could understand. We labelled them too easily. We said that he was impatient and always had to be the centre of attention. One afternoon when Mum's sister turned up on a quiet Saturday, he stormed out of the house without saying a word to her. He went to the races and lost a bomb. We said that he would only associate with his kids when we succeeded. He never showed up to our sports events because we were nearly always the worst players on the worst teams, but he always came to the academic prize-giving where we did well. We said he was proud. Once, when he'd had a long spell in hospital, we saved up to buy him a walking stick to help him get around and he reacted with wounded indignation.

'He doesn't drink,' Mum said often, as much to herself as to us. 'And he doesn't see strange women.'

As well as fidelity, Dad did have another gift. He was capable of seeing himself, even if only in glimpses. One day I managed to figure out how to open his Gladstone bag. It had a tricky lock. Inside was nothing but an old exercise book. In the exercise book, there were columns of figures entered in his large, mannered handwriting in fountain pen. Beside some of the figures were dates and beside others the names of places: Randwick, Warwick Farm, Rosehill. These were his gambling expenses, each loss carefully noted so it could stare back at him.

I was with him once when he decided to drop in to a pharmacy in Crows Nest. He moved uneasily up and down in front of the counter, eyeing the Pirofin that was on a shelf where you had to ask for it. He waited until every customer had gone before catching the eye of the pharmacist. Then other customers came in and he told her to serve them first. We waited. It seemed like a long time. He looked at perfumes and presents he might buy for Mum. He was wrestling with himself.

Eventually he stood at the counter and said a single word.

'Pirofin.'

He sounded defeated.

~

Dad was not bad but trapped. Even as a kid I realised this somewhere deep and sore. Once we'd been out to see a friend of Mum's in hospital who'd just given birth. I can't remember if she'd had a baby or an infant. We parked and went inside. It was a hot day and Dad was edgy. He kept asking Mum if she wanted a cup of tea. Mum didn't. Dad insisted that she did. Mum insisted that she didn't. Finally, we walked a long distance to find a cafe in which Mum could, in Dad's words, sit down, relax and have a nice cup of tea. When we got there, Dad wanted some powders and orange juice. He had several powders one on top of the other. Then, no sooner had Mum's tea arrived than Dad wanted to leave. He kept rushing her. She scalded her lips. Dad was angry that she was so slow. She burnt her throat and ended up leaving half the tea behind. I knew then that Dad had a problem. He was desperate to leave the scene of another defeat.

Once I asked Dad why he needed the Pirofin.

He thought for a while.

'It gives me a lift,' he said plainly.

Years later I had to contend with depression and compulsive behaviour myself. I understood Dad better.

When you're seriously depressed, you are locked out of yourself. You can watch yourself sitting in front of a gaming machine stuffing a week's salary mindlessly into the slot, and it's like you're watching somebody else. You can watch yourself drinking, eating, being promiscuous, buying forty pairs of shoes, unable to pick up the phone. You can even watch yourself crying. You're like a kid locked out of their house without a key. Your house is burning and there's no way you can get back inside to rescue the things you love.

Dad is getting back into Mum's car. He has just met his brother. The brother is brilliant, mercurial. He was dux of the school and a translator during the war. He had a mystique, even as a kid. His mother held up the family table when he wanted to speak, although possibly he only wanted to say that he quite liked stewed apples. He came unstuck as an adult. He was sick. He did things. We didn't know exactly what. It was whispered that he'd burnt down his own house. Mum worried for us when his name was in the paper for a crime he was alleged to have committed.

Dad meets him in a park. They talk. Dad gets back into the car. He says his brother is coming over to say hello. Mum stiffens. We are allowed to wind down the window one inch and say our names. We may not shake hands. We may call him Uncle. We may not get out of the car.

Thirteen

THERE IS MORE, miles more, to healing than pills. Heading north in England, we called on some friends who lived in Chester. They run a small hotel just outside the old Roman walls. They regaled us with stories about running the business and I began to feel a bit more sympathy for Eliot, the proprietor of Bath. Ann and Viv, however, told their stories with a lightness of touch. They believed that the right place for a chip was in the fryer and not on your shoulder.

Ann took Mum and me across the border into Wales. Our destination was St Winefride's Well. I'm not much of an enthusiast for Fatima and such places. The sign that welcomed us to 'The Lourdes of Wales' put me on my guard, as did the showroom with a familiar range of religious kitsch, as did the warning against bringing dogs onto the site. I've known dogs as much in need of miraculous healing as their owners. But I have always liked graffiti. In the stonework around the well has been carved the name of a traveller and the simple message *Cured 1831*. I don't know why vandalism speaks to me more powerfully than all the postcards and holy medals that ever gathered dust in the bottom of drawers, but in this case it did. The mother of Henry VII (one of the last of 'our' monarchs) built a chapel over the well around 1500, and the crypt is riddled with the graffiti which testifies to centuries of hopeful travel to this place.

The legend is that in AD 660 St Winefride was martyred on this spot when she refused to surrender her virginity to the son of Caradoc, a local prince. It's easy to mistake the stories of Christian virgins for stories of sexual reserve; in fact, most of them are stories of the refusal to hand over power. This one certainly is. It was a brave young woman who resisted the attentions of Caradoc. They say that the spring arose where her severed head hit the ground: another story of blood mixed with water. Mum drank some of the water, which was somewhat rash for her, and within half an hour declared her hay fever cured. But she was still a pharmacist. We bought some little plastic medicine bottles to take the water home. It may have been miraculous but it still needed a lid and a label.

St Winefride's uncle was called St Beuno. There is a large Jesuit house named after him nearby. It is now a retreat centre, but it was designed in 1843 by the Hansom of Hansom Cab notoriety soon after the restoration of Catholicism in Britain, as a place for young Jesuits to study theology. Its most famous resident was the poet Gerard Manley Hopkins. Hopkins was another post-office Catholic; he became a convert after an exchange of letters with Newman in the 1860s. It was while he lived at Beuno's that his superior got him to do himself a favour and start taking seriously his interest in poetry. His long work, 'The Wreck of the Deutschland', was written here. It's a poem about nuns killed at sea written from the safe harbour of *I in my cell*. Hopkins' whole life was lived on the sidelines a bit like that. He was the kind of Jesuit whose superiors never knew quite where to put.

We stood in the chapel in which he was ordained. In the refectory, you can still see the pulpit in which Hopkins was laughed at by his fellow students when he was trying to deliver a sermon. It was once the custom for Jesuits to thunder down sermons not just in church but also over dinner. Hopkins tried to compare the valley below St Beuno's with the Holy Land, but made the mistake of stretching the analogy to include every minor geographical landmark. Part of his audience began giggling. Before long the whole room was trying to contain itself. Hopkins was unable to continue. He had to step down. But he had the last laugh. His ridiculous homily has been carefully included in Hopkins' collected works which are now revered in the St Beuno's library. One of his most famous sermons compared the church to a sow, in which each of the seven sacraments corresponded to one of its seven teats. He was ungainly.

Except when it came to poetry. Here he was as bruised and determined as a rugby scrum half:

> *I am at once what Christ is, since he was what I*
> *am, and*
> *This Jack, joke, poor potsherd, patch, match-*
> *wood, immortal diamond,*
> *Is immortal diamond.*

~

By the time we got back to Chester, Ann had developed a nasty corn on her foot. She regretted not having put it in St Winefride's Well.

Mum said she had the answer. I expected her to return with some of Winefride's water, but instead she dug into her cosmetic case and produced a small metal canister. I recognised it at once. This is where she keeps her Baxter's Ointment. I have always thought that Mum invented Baxter's Ointment. After all, it bears her name and I've never known anybody else who has either heard of it or used it. But Mum stoutly denies the achievement. When we were young, Baxter's Ointment was solemnly produced on the occasion of every splinter, every ant bite, every wart, every inexplicable mole or blemish. It always works. It's incredible. Mum says it has the ability to draw poisons and other foreign substances out of the body. She won't say how it does this but I've long been at a loss to know why such a potent force for good is not available on the pharmaceutical market when you can readily buy half a dozen anti-fungal powders in which you can grow anything from tinea to mushrooms.

The recipe for Baxter's Ointment has always been a closely guarded secret. As a young woman, Mum was the sole person in Rose's Pharmacy entrusted with its preparation. It contained zinc oxide, boracic acid, resin ointment and olive oil. The legendary Australian cricketer Richie Benaud used a similar preparation to ease the damage done to his fingers by spin bowling. Part of the difference between Baxter's Ointment and calamine or anything else is the difference between a print and an original. The Baxter's was always made by hand for every customer. It was a work of art. The customer often had to come back the next day to allow time for its proper distillation. When Mum left Rose's forty years ago, she took with her enough Baxter's Ointment to embalm a horse. It was still treated as precious. In times of need, it was dug out of the back of the bathroom cupboard and a tiny smear was applied to the pad of a bandaid. Another bandaid was put over the top of this to make sure the first one didn't fall off and waste the ointment. Every year, for forty years, Mum has added a little olive oil to the ointment to stop it drying out. On the other side of the world, she produced part of the same batch of Baxter's Ointment which she had taken with her from Rose's. A few days later, we rang Ann from Glasgow to check on the progress of the foot.

'That stuff of your mother's is miraculous,' she said.

Which now only left me scratching my head about the need to break the customs laws and smuggle Winefride's water into Australia.

Fourteen

FOR ME, HOPKINS is a kind of family member. One I'd wanted to look up. The further north we got, the more Mum started listening for traces of the accent of her father, John Baxter. In the Lakes district, we spent a morning at Dove Cottage, the place where the poet Wordsworth earned the laurels which he spent so many years sitting on. In the garden, Mum stopped and looked twice before she recognised a gooseberry bush. She told me that gooseberry pie was her father's favourite. He travelled the world but loved nothing more than his own garden, his own gooseberry bush, his own gooseberry pie.

In Glasgow, Mum was a young woman again. When we found ourselves in a noisy bar, full of passionate fans watching the broadcast of Scotland's last-ditch bid to stay alive in the Euro 96, she thought she could get the publican to turn off the TV. I didn't think so. Next day, we made for the ancient cathedral and the St Mungo Museum of Religious Life and Art, which is in the cathedral's precincts. The pride and joy of the museum is Salvador Dali's *Christ of St John of the Cross*. The problem with the St Mungo Museum, much like any gallery which has only one really famous painting, is that every postcard, poster, placard and pointer to the museum features a reproduction of the painting, so that by the time you actually get there you have long since become sick of the sight of it.

Strangely, the thirteenth-century cathedral is now thought of as adjoining the modern museum, not the other way round. We went there second. Miss Grey, the volunteer guide who conducted us through the cathedral, seemed appropriately named. She warned us, too late, against setting foot in the museum. She spent much of the time pointing a bony finger at some architectural feature but telling us about the horrors of the museum.

'It may be very nice, but you won't see very much Christian there.'

Any place where there were no fewer than 50 000 images of Christ on the premises, admittedly *à la* Dali, was hardly lacking in Christian iconography, but I gathered she was referring to the various items of Hindu headwear, Bahai bathwear and Jewish jewellery which fill the gaps between the reproductions of Dali.

Nevertheless, Miss Grey was delighted by the refurbished organ which had just been transplanted into the cathedral.

'I've left my organs to medical science,' said an American who'd joined our little party.

'Yes,' replied Mum, 'but do your organs sound as good as Miss Grey's?'

~

In Fort William, the furthest north we went, we shared haggis in a pub that had been making it according to the same recipe since the turn of the nineteenth century. Haggis does not bear much detailed description except for the observation that whoever thought of using intestines as the tubing for a sausage may have had an eye for economy but also did a lot to earn the Scots their reputation for pinching pennies. Haggis is normally served with turnips, a vegetable of which I have a low opinion.

'But surely you had turnips at home,' said Mum.

'What do you mean?'

I thought Mum would remember what we had at home.

'Didn't Katie used to cook them for you?'

'There was no Katie ever cooked for us.'

'At Sunray.'

The penny dropped for me just as Mum was waking from a kind of daydream. She had been talking to me as if I were Dad. Sunray was the name of the house he grew up in. She apologised, but there was no need.

Fifteen

IN EDINBURGH, we made our way slowly down the Royal Mile. On one short stretch have lived (not all at the same time) the likes of Robert Burns, Robert Louis Stevenson, Tobias Smollett, Adam Smith, David Hume, James Boswell, John Knox and numerous unrelated John Baxters.

One of the Mile's attractions is the way that the most numbing trivia sit side by side with the most breathtaking history. You can buy kilts to take home for your dog, your cat, even your pet mice. I spent a brief time in one antiquarian book shop, just long enough to overhear a visitor specify the book she was looking for. She wanted something in leather and it had to be a certain size to fit the space she had left in her luggage for it. It also had to be a certain colour to match her furnishings.

'Does the subject matter matter?' asked the seller.

'As long as it won't embarrass any visitors.'

The Royal Mile has done a lot more for literature than provide ornamental editions. Never was a better flesh creeper put to paper than *The Strange Case of Dr Jekyll and Mr Hyde*. It's one of those books which has been sadly trivialised as Hollywood schlock. Its real horror is that it is so mundane. It's a book about taking a few pills. Dr Jekyll manipulates drugs to escape his own personality and slip into that of Mr Hyde. The story deals with issues which burn in every contemporary pharmacy as well as my own life. As time goes by, Jekyll is increasingly trapped by the drugs. He becomes dependent on the alter ego of Mr Hyde, within which he hides himself. It's not just a psychological story; it's a story about substance and substance abuse.

To step from a shop where you can get a 'St Andrews' golf ball personalised with your own initials into the very premises once occupied by Deacon William Brodie is like stepping from a putting green into the long grass. Brodie was Robert Louis Stevenson's model for the characterisation of both Jekyll and Hyde. He was a cabinet maker by day and a burglar by night, a feat he achieved by keeping copies of the keys of the shops he worked in. He was also a city councillor by day and a drinker and gambler by night, although it's harder to get modern people to see this as a dichotomy. When he was finally caught, the public was so horrified that such a quiet and steady citizen was capable of this that his punishment was tough. He was not a freak in the way many criminals are to those on the right side of the bars; he was too much like one of them. He was hanged on October 1, 1788. The gallows on which he was hanged were ones which he had made himself.

I could talk for ages about Stevenson, one of the most complex characters ever to have tried the guise of a simple story teller. He happened to be in Sydney in 1890, when he noticed a letter in the paper complaining about a Belgian

Catholic monk called Father Damien. This was the well known Damien of Molokai who had lived and died among victims of leprosy in a remote island in the Hawaiian group. Stevenson had only recently returned from Molokai and had his own views about the work Damien had done. Nevertheless, he might never have noticed the letter in the paper except for the name of the signatory. It was Hyde. Stevenson responded by writing a long and passionate vindication of Damien. He was reaching across cultural and religious stereotypes to a priest whose humanity Stevenson understood better than his theology.

Stevenson wrote a book called *Travels with a Donkey in the Cevennes*, the result of a twelve-day journey he made on foot though the Cevennes ranges in France in 1878. He spent several nights at inns, several sleeping out and one in a Trappist monastery. He packed a lot of gear, including a revolver, books to read and an egg whisk which he needed to prepare the egg-and-brandy drink which was his regular morning heart-starter. Stevenson did not intend to carry this stuff himself. His companion on the trip was a donkey called Modestine. Modestine was only partially co-operative. In fact, she was on heat for most of the journey. This was not inappropriate as Stevenson was thinking about sex a lot himself. At the time, Stevenson was beginning to court Fanny Osbourne, a much older woman, married with children, who was to become his companion on future journeys. Stevenson, alone, was deeply exercised along the way by religious longings, religious nostalgia. He says: *we are all travellers in what John Bunyan calls this wilderness of the world . . . the best we can find in our travels is an honest friend.*

Stevenson ended his days in Samoa. Poor health had forced him to move to a warmer climate. His mother decided to follow him there. Like so many of the figures who took my eye on our travels, Stevenson had an interesting relationship with his mother. When Mrs Stevenson senior finally got to Apia she had thirty-eight shipping cases. She had brought with her every item of the heavy, dark Victorian furniture from her home in Scotland, as well as a supply of 'widow's weeds' sufficient to last the rest of her life. So, in the tropics, Stevenson started reading in a stiff, upholstered armchair. The family now ate between the slat walls of a weatherboard house with no doors, sitting around a massive mahogany dining table.

The preface of *Travels with a Donkey* includes a famous statement:

> *every book is, in an intimate sense, a circular letter to the friends of him who writes it. They alone take his meaning; they find private messages, assurances of love and expressions of gratitude dropped at every corner. The public is but a generous patron who defrays the postage.*

It's curious that Stevenson calls his book a 'circular letter' because all circles lead back home. When I was at university, I studied literature with people who seemed so frightened by what had been entrusted to them that they lived by denial. They said things like 'there is no such thing as a text' and 'the author is dead'. They often used the metaphor of land or landscape to describe a written work, but treated those works as subject to no prior claim, *terra nullius*. In the same breath they would lament the injustice by which the first Europeans to settle Australia treated the land as *terra nullius*. I couldn't figure this out. To me these readers were like theologians who feel the need to deny the existence of God so their subject matter can be kept down to a size they can handle. From them, I gleaned a sense that reading was like visiting an empty house. Books were haunted: they were made of ghostly presences, shades which passed through in their restless wanderings beyond the grave.

I am a different reader from the one I was when I was a kid with my nose stuck in books during the holidays. I don't see reading as a form of escape or flight but as a form of hospitality. I have come to believe that literature is not haunted. It is inhabited. A reader never travels alone. Reading Austen or Hopkins or Wordsworth or the Brontës or Newman is doing more than defraying their postage. It's paying the mortgage on a place for yourself to live, a place from which you can open the door to other travellers.

Sixteen

YOU CAN SEE THE FUTURE. Also hear it. Sight and sound allow you to see a car coming in the distance or hear a storm moving in on you. On the other hand, you can only touch things in the present; it's hard to have a relationship of any closeness without touch. Grief is an experience of touch; it sits in your bowels.

But taste and smell enable you to sense the past. They are the most immediate and infallible triggers of memory. In Edinburgh, we found our way into a duty-free store and tried a few fragrances. Suddenly Mum smiled. She had recognised something. She sprayed some perfume on my wrist, then a bit more. The attendant eyed us cautiously. It was one of the most expensive in the range and we were using it like fly spray.

'That was my mother's perfume,' Mum said, as we were shown the door. 'It was the only one she ever wore. The minute she walked into a room everybody smelt it and knew – Linda had arrived.'

I got the impression that Mum's mother, Linda, was a woman in the mould of Lady Bracknell. Mum invariably described Linda as 'poised and refined' and since Mum usually only expresses displeasure in duplicate, I wonder if these words have a slight unconscious edge. Linda had been a parlour boarder at St Vincent's, Potts Point, in the first decade of the century. Here she had learnt the right way to sit, the right way to hold a cup and saucer and the right way to refuse an unwelcome proposal of marriage. We had a photo at home of Linda and her class mates, looking demure and wearing as much lace and frills as would these days outfit the clientele of an entire disco. But they were bodily women. Mum said that when Linda got married she had an eighteen-inch waist. She knew that. They must have discussed such things. In the photo, however, butter wouldn't melt in their armpits. They were the Catholic ladies of the future, straining their future out of a teapot. I often wondered how Linda hit it off with John Baxter, the seaman from Newcastle, and how she coped in her later years when illness forced her to wear a glass eye.

Growing up, we heard one story about Linda. We heard it often but it was one that, often as she threatened, Mum would never emulate. When Mum was a child, Linda was unimpressed with her table manners. She waited until some of Mum's friends came around to eat. Linda dug her elbows into the table, chomped with her mouth open, and put on an ugly performance imitating Mum's etiquette. Mum was humiliated. She often said she would improve our manners by doing the same for us. This was her worst threat, delivered with feeling. But she never did. She had been hurt. The thing about Mum is that you have to put together a lot of small pieces to find that out.

I learnt more about Mum's family when she was

talking to Trixie in London than I had on my own. Mum told her that, when her parents first married, John Baxter wouldn't have a picture of the Sacred Heart hanging in the house. He was proud to be what he called a 'Caluthumpian', which meant more than that he had no religion. It meant that he thought religion was a load of hogwash. Neighbours would see him doing something in his garden, his real church, on their way to their church on a Sunday morning and chastise him for working on the Sabbath.

'Better the day, better the deed,' he said with contempt.

When he refused to hang the Sacred Heart, Linda walked out on him. That must have taken guts in those days. He came running after her.

Mum also said that her mother had had a falling out with her own mother because Linda wanted to go to a fancy dress party as Joan of Arc. I wondered what on earth could be wrong about that. Joan of Arc was a saint and, therefore, surely the perfect model to copy. The problem was that Joan of Arc dressed like a man. She wore armour and carried a sword. So to dress up as St Joan you had to dress as a man and that was an absolute no-no. But Linda did it anyway. And she had herself photographed. Mum still has the photo. Another time, Linda was asked to be a bridesmaid at the wedding of a non-Catholic. This was considered another unspeakable crime against humanity. But Linda worked on the principle of 'act first and ask questions later'. I relished these stories of a woman who'd made up her own mind about religion and wasn't going to be bullied by either believers or unbelievers.

Trixie said that she knew Linda for a long time before she discovered that she was a warm woman. Her earliest recollections of her are sitting in the front row of the school theatre and looking formidable. It took a while for her other side to thaw. But it did. Photographs of Linda have survived but not many stories. Stories tell far more than photos. A photo is a single image. A story passes through the hands of dozens, sometimes hundreds, of tellers and you learn something from them all.

~

One day, Mum was cleaning up at home. She produced an envelope with affected casualness. It obviously contained something precious to her and she wanted to protect the vulnerability needed to show me whatever it was, in case I was off-hand about it. Inside, was a small piece of paper held together with a pin and inside the paper were two or three dried petals marked *From the rose of St Therese*. They had long since lost their fragrance. Next to this was a medal which featured on one side an image of Jesus known as the Sacred Heart. On the other side was a picture of Mary, the mother of Jesus, standing with open arms. This type of devotional item is known as a 'miraculous medal'. It had been placed on a red ribbon, now fading, and in the ribbon a neat press-stud had been sewn by hand. With the medal came a note:

> *My darling,*
> *If you should come across this little parcel you may wonder why but it is so the mother of God*

may always watch over you that I am putting it in
your pocket. Don't lose it. The medal is blessed.
  Linda
PS Not the medal look after you, but the mother
of God.

Linda had slipped the envelope into John's pocket
when he returned to sea in the last days of World War I,
immediately after they were married. She had already
lost one sweetheart to the war and didn't want to lose
another. John and Linda were married in September
1918; the war ended in November. That still left time for
tragedy to visit. After all, the poet Wilfred Owen was
killed only days before the armistice came into effect.
Apparently, in those months, John was on a ship which
got lost because it missed the lighthouse at the entrance
of New York harbour. To miss such an obvious landmark
was a sign of gross incompetence for any navigator. But
every other ship which made sighting of the lighthouse
that night was torpedoed and sunk. So the story goes.

On the outside of the envelope the same hand, now
much older, has written:

In here is the medal of the Sacred Heart of Jesus.
He brought John back to me. He was away two
and a half years.

Seventeen

A FEW WEEKS AFTER we had been in Britain, Mum and I embarked upon the second of our packaged bus tours in Europe. This was the one that took us through five countries in seven days and which we signed up for because we got a hundred-dollar discount. It turned out to be an orchestrated series of shopping opportunities. We spent twenty-four hours in Germany, most of it being shown bargain-priced cuckoo clocks. We found our way into a German cafe where the menu had pasted into it the labels from the tins of soup that you could order, much like other places have labels from bottles of fine wine. In Lucerne, we were shown what was said to be the world's most expensive watch shop. One watch was ticketed at $68 000 and another at $72 000. But each came with a twelve-month guarantee.

On the way back to England, the bus skirted through the north of France at breakneck speed. Being on a freeway is much like flying. You don't really connect with the country you're breezing over. Roads used to string places together; freeways bypass them. Freeways in Australia have effectively buried entire communities from sight.

Both Mum and I had seen plenty of pictures of these fields that were around us now in the north of France. Always black-and-white. Most showed untold destruction and vast expanses of mud. Generally with human remains littered around them. Linda's first fiancé was killed somewhere nearby. On a sweet morning in July 1996, we passed the River Somme at 110 km/h; there were 60 000 casualties here on a single day in July, 1916. Kitchener's territorials had been, as the name implies, recruited by locations. So at intervals of ten or fifteen minutes, the entire working male population of cities such as Liverpool was annihilated, suburb by suburb, street by street. Ironically, nothing could honour that kind of mindlessness more poignantly than the banality of a freeway.

We stopped for coffee at a roadhouse, one of those large, anonymous places which stand as victors where you used to see towns. Their neon signs grin idiotically at the passing traffic they want to entice. Everybody went inside and I took the chance to wander about forty or fifty metres from where the bus was parked. Within a minute I had kicked over the fractured casing of a twenty-four-inch artillery shell. It had been there for eighty years. Such discoveries are by no means unusual. In 1993 alone, 90 tonnes of metal were collected from the fields of France by the Mine Clearance Service. In 1991, thirty-six farmers were killed when they stumbled across unexploded weaponry. Every year, half a dozen mine disposal experts are killed as they go about the endless task of restoring the countryside. In 1991 and 1992, as the line was created for the TGV – the fast train that connects London and Paris – the mine disposal crews worked on the Somme around the clock. This was the route of the train. They collected five tonnes of shells a day. The stuff keeps working its way to the surface like car tyres do in a rubbish dump.

The one shell I kicked over put a lump in my throat. It was mighty heavy. I said a prayer for whoever it may have killed, another for whoever fired it, then knocked the dirt off it and sneaked it into my baggage. I watched the poor handler at Calais lug the bag onto the hydrofoil and, somehow or other, we managed to get it as far as London. Trixie and Kevin probably wonder what they did to be suddenly lumbered with this unwieldy garden ornament. The artillery shell was a thousand times the weight of Linda's miraculous medal.

I can't deal with the question of why God would choose to save someone because they were wearing a medal and let three or four other ships sink on their way to New York. Or why Linda's first fiancé was killed in World War I and John Baxter was not. Or why something as destructive as an artillery shell should become a banal part of a banal landscape in which neon signs scream about the price of a cup of coffee. They are similar questions to the ones which defeated me at the end of my pilgrimage with Peter. Why would providence be so good to me and let others starve? But a question, however troubling, is one thing; gratitude is another. Mary MacKillop said that gratitude is the memory of the heart. However remote I feel from the piety which would secretly slip a holy medal into the pocket of your agnostic beloved, I am certainly heir to the gratitude which Linda expressed on the outside of that envelope. It is the basis of what faith I have.

When I think of Dad, he is pale and breathless. He is stunned and he looks like he's been hit. He is getting back into the car. He is holding his hat. He rolls the brim gently like a cigarette paper. It is Christmas, eighteen months since his mother died. We have been driving down town for carols. On the freeway, he looks across to the gate of his old family home, 'Sunray'. The house has been standing empty for some time. He sees people going in through the gate. Strangers. Carrying stuff. We go back. Dad goes in alone. He comes back. There are squatters in the family home. They have stripped the ceilings of lead. They've lit fires to cook. They've made a mess. There's water damage. They have moved into Dad's private world, into his childhood. They have told him to piss off. Mum says he is not going back into the house without the police.

Eighteen

I WAS WRONG ABOUT TOUCH. You can also touch the past.

In each new city we got on the local guided bus tour. In Glasgow we had a mountain of fun because the guide was so cynical about his own city. He told us that the architects of modern Glasgow had worked so rapidly and with such enthusiasm that they paused only to feed their guide dogs. He said they should be grateful that all the old sub-standard housing, which so many people associated with Glasgow, had been replaced by new sub-standard housing. He pointed out the original 'paddy's market' where Irish refugees literally sold the shirts off their backs; he then indicated our group and said it was nice to see the riff-raff still finding their way to Glasgow. Finally we paused in front of the modern arts centre. Every decent-sized city has one of these. Indecent-sized cities might have two or three. No matter how ugly they are, they must always be spoken of in awed terms by the loyal citizens who forked out the money without being consulted about whether they really wanted staircases shaped like corkscrews, ceilings like wine glasses and walls in the colours of a bad hangover. In Glasgow the guide simply told us he would pause for two minutes' silence in front of their arts centre.

'I can't find a word to say about it,' he said.

The next guide, in Edinburgh, fitted the stereotypical image of that city as much as the one had in Glasgow. She was dour, serious, dressed in a twin-set and alarmingly well informed. The driver had to hold up traffic for three blocks while she went through absolutely everything she knew about a local landmark. Once a city has been in the same location for more than a thousand years, some abridgement is called for, I think. But the guide didn't think so, except in one particular. To do her justice, she had lighted upon one surprisingly effective form of verbal economy. Unlike her fellow countrymen, the comedian Billy Connolly and novelist James Kelman, she seemed able to describe things other than as 'fucking'. Edinburgh is obviously a more chaste city than Glasgow. The Glaswegian guide had urged us to look at the fucking town hall, admire a fucking bridge and applaud some fucking thing by Charles Rennie fucking Mackintosh. But the guide in Edinburgh did not use this word, even when pointing to a statue of Edward VII about whom it may have been appropriate.

Finally we came to a statue of one of the prime ministers, Pitt. This was where Mum might have been expected to use the f word, except that she never does. I knew in advance what she was going to say.

'Is that Pitt the Younger or Pitt the Elder?'

We got an answer but I can't remember what it was.

Mum chuckled. When she was in the middle of high school, she was thrown out of history class for not knowing the difference between the Pitt the Younger and Pitt the Elder. She went out the door with her books behind her, followed a split second later by her school bag. Once Mother Somebody had tossed you out, there was no redress. So Mum had to give up history, and take up chemistry. All because she'd failed one round of trivial pursuit. Mother Somebody, much revered, was feeding her students junk food: filling their heads with meaningless facts and figures and killing their appetite in the meantime. The whole point of teaching is to uncover questions. Tolstoy said that *a thought can propel your life in the right direction only when it answers questions asked by your soul.* In other words, nobody gets interested in the answers to questions which, wherever they may have originated, have not become their own.

∼

As we edged out of Edinburgh, the weather closed around us. It was so cold and wet at the English border that only the bikies were braving the elements: the rest of the travellers stayed in their cars and nursed thermos flasks. We pushed on slowly towards Newcastle, the place John Baxter had left in a hurry.

Something happened on the way to Newcastle which showed that Mum was carrying a question of her own. The rain stopped and the sun started beating against the windscreen. I complained vigorously that these silly rented cars never have air conditioning. I pulled over to take off my pullover. Mum got a bit tearful. I thought I must have upset her by whingeing, so I started to apologise.

'It just gets a bit hot, that's all. I'm sorry.'

Mum then began to cry. But it was nothing to do with

me. She blew her nose and told me simply that before she left Australia she had said to God that if the sun was shining when she got to Newcastle, she would know that her father was in heaven. As we drove through the outskirts, Mum closed her eyes contentedly. She had found out what she wanted to know. Her father's current address.

Nineteen

MUM, LIKE MYSELF, is a tactile historian. Tactile historians wrestle with the past. The past isn't something to know about; it's something to get hold of. It's an explanation, not a random set of incidents. Mum's question about where John had gone suggested that something about him was unresolved in her mind.

The hotel we stayed at in Newcastle-on-Tyne was once a mansion, perhaps the property of a ship owner. Although it was now somewhat down-at-heel, it indicated that, away from the docks, there had been a salubrious end of town. The people who ran the hotel had gone away for the weekend, leaving an elderly relative in charge. Ena told us that Newcastle was very much a young person's town. A lot of the industry, especially the shipyards, had been emasculated but young people came from all over Yorkshire and the north just to go to the night-clubs in Newcastle. Ena's boyfriend opened the bar in the early evening and we were joined by two fellow guests, both women, both in their late forties. One of their sons, aged twenty, had just landed himself an apprenticeship. This was apparently a rare achievement in the north. So they had left their men folk at home and come into Newcastle to kick up their heels. The heels they were preparing to kick up looked suitably dangerous.

'Mutton dressed as lamb,' said Mum, when we went upstairs.

'What do you mean?'

'Those two. They should dress their age.'

'I guess so.'

'They'll break an ankle in those shoes.'

'I suppose so.'

'Then they'll be satisfied.'

'Come on, Mum. What do you want to do now?'

'I think we should stay here and have an early night.'

'But we still have three hours of daylight.'

'I think we need a rest.'

'But this is your father's town. Don't you want to have a look at it?'

'Maybe tomorrow.'

'What do you mean, *maybe*?'

'I don't know.'

Pause.

'Is there any way we could find where your father used to live?'

Mum fell silent again. She was wrestling with something in her mind.

Five minutes later, she was back to digging in her suitcase. She probed the inmost zippered pockets. Eventually she put her hand on an old wallet and handed it to me without comment. It is a simple piece of work: unostentatious but solid. I began looking inside. It was empty. No money.

'There's nothing in here.'

'Read it.'

'How do you read a wallet?'

'Read what's stamped in the leather.'

On the bill-fold inside was printed in gold letters: *John Baxter, 26 Simonside Terrace, Heaton-on-Tyne.* Enough to go on.

Twenty

JOHN BAXTER SENIOR, Mum's grandfather, had eleven children. Mum's father was the eldest and inherited the name of his old man. Neither of them had a second name: they were just John Baxter.

The father and son didn't hit it off. I asked Mum if it were just possible that the wallet had belonged first to her grandfather and been given to the son. She said there was no way that could have happened. There was no way her father would have taken anything from the old man. All he ever accepted from him was a fob watch. He was marking time till he could get away. He didn't like the way his father, who was a merchant, spent hours drinking whisky with business people but didn't seem to have any time for his own family. John Junior may have been a smoker from the age of nine, but he never touched grog. He never once sat at the same dining table as his father.

John Junior took his exams and was certified as a first-class marine engineer in 1909. He left Newcastle before the outbreak of World War I, before emigration became difficult. He took a risk. This was the era which built the *Lusitania*, the *Normandie* and *Titanic*. The shipyards were humming and John was highly qualified. Britain relied heavily on its navy. John had real prospects. But none of that stacked up against the need for John to leave the orbit of his father.

His biggest regret was that he never returned to England to see his mother, Maggie Clark. One night, many years later, his wife Linda woke him to describe a woman she'd seen standing at the foot of their bed as he slept. You would have expected John Baxter to have been dismissive of such tomfoolery. His attitude to spirituality was pretty concrete, symbolised by the tool bag of the Freemasons which he had taken to meetings in Newcastle and which gathered dust in the back of his wardrobe in Australia. But on this occasion, John didn't go into the back room for a smoke or do something practical in the kitchen. He listened to Linda's description of the woman in their room.

'That's my mother,' he said simply in his soft Geordie voice.

Two days later they got word from the other side of the world that Maggie was dead.

This experience, I suspect, marks the beginning of change in John. He was softening. I'd love to know what he did next, how he handled his grief and whether or not he chose to speak to anybody about his loss. I feel some affinity with a man who inadvertently made his mother pay the price of his problems with his father. John packed his kit bag and went to sea in a similar frame of mind to that with which I entered the Jesuits.

John was lucky to have Linda. She was far more sure of herself than her husband. John was a closet sentimentalist. One of Mum's earliest memories is of walking over the Sydney Harbour Bridge with her mother and sister on the day it opened, while her father stayed at home. Sixty years later, she rekindled the experience by being one of the thousands who walked the length of the new Sydney Harbour Tunnel on the day *that* opened. The bridge is a kind of family icon. It was opened by Jack Lang, the political sparring partner of Dad's dad. I went to school within sight of it and loved the occasional foggy morning you get in Sydney when it looked like the bridge had disappeared. It was on the bridge that I told Mum I was joining the order; it was the bridge which, for years, joined home to Sydney Hospital where Dad was a patient.

For John Baxter, Sydney Harbour Bridge was only ever an imitation of the bridge on the Tyne at Newcastle. He was an engineer so this was given as a professional judgement. The same firms had been responsible for both projects, but John definitely preferred Newcastle's. He referred to it often and Mum passed the comparison on to us as kids. Yet on our arrival in Newcastle, one of the first things that dawned on us was that the bridge in Newcastle had been opened in 1927. This meant John Baxter had never laid eyes on it: he had left town before the first foundations were sunk. In other words, he was inordinately proud of a bridge he had not even seen. This, to me, is the measure of the nostalgia he felt. When a Geordie engineer starts talking about a bridge, you could be listening to an account of homesickness.

~

We were surprised how easy it was to locate the house at 26 Simonside Terrace. Mum had brought with her photos of her English grandparents taking their leisure in the gardens of a handsome property, with a fine-looking dog in the background. I think this was the kind of place we expected to find. But Simonside Terrace is a long row of narrow tenements. Houses have been pushed and shoved to fit in like people filling the back row of a photo. Mum and I both decided instantaneously that this was not the family home at all. It was far too small to accommodate eleven children, let alone any help, and bore absolutely no resemblance to the lifestyle implied in the long-cherished photos Mum had with her. Indeed, the whole of Heaton was chequered with hundreds and hundreds of these look-alike houses.

We thought, on the face of it, that this must be the place that John Baxter lived in when he first moved out of home. This would explain why he so proudly had the address embossed on his wallet: both the wallet and the house are signs of independence. Besides, the place looks like ideal student digs. Somebody had painted the door a bright, lurid red. The little entrance porch over the doors of most places in the street had fallen away. The garden was the size of a pocket handkerchief and a complete mess, a state John Baxter, the seaman who loved his garden, would have found intolerable. There was junk-food litter and an abandoned Ventolin inhaler among the weedy undergrowth. The window frames were beginning to rot.

'Let's take a photo,' I suggested.

'Take a photo of the place a few doors down.'

'Why?'

'That one's been looked after better. The garden looks nice.'

'Yes, but it wasn't your father's place.'

'There's no number on the door of that one. You couldn't tell.'

'But it's not the actual place.'

'Every place in the street looks the same.'

'But not every place *is* the same.'

Outside, we ran into a young man called David. David was going from door to door selling subscriptions to cable television. He spoke to the people in 22, who weren't interested, then to the ones in 24, who weren't interested either. Then he spoke to us. He was excited to meet us, not because we had a connection with the next door he was due to door-knock, but because his dream was to emigrate to Australia. He had been told that Australia was a land of great opportunity. He wanted to go out there and become a full-time soccer coach; he'd heard that they were employing coaches virtually as they stepped off the plane. I didn't want to prick his illusion; besides, Mum had fallen in love with his Geordie accent. It was possible to believe that we'd turned back the clock ninety years and were speaking to the young John Baxter, bursting with dreams and energy and desperate to get out of Newcastle. Mum even told David that her father loved soccer, which was news to me. Ironically, David was saving to make more room for himself in the world by selling cable on the promise that the connection would make the world smaller and render travel obsolete, even to the shops.

Simonside Terrace, on our only night in Newcastle, was neither the time nor the place to argue the fine points of global communications. David had another door to knock. It was number 26. He said that he would knock and when the residents answered he would explain who we were and ask them if we could have a look inside. Sounded great. But of course, there was nobody home. We waited. No luck.

It was time for David to knock off. We got him to take our photo standing in front of 26.

'Only an idiot would paint a front door that colour,' said Mum.

'I'll start here again in the morning,' David said, getting into a small car which had pulled up for him. There were already five other beefy telecommunications salesmen in the little car. They didn't look a cheery mob. They all worked on commission.

Mum and I took a walk around into the right-of-way at the back of the row. There was a pile of junk at the back of number 26 and, on top of the lot, an old TV aerial had been discarded. Whoever now lived at 26 Simonside Terrace had had their communications revolution already. Some young men yelled something indistinguishable at us from the end of the lane. There were needles lying between the paving stones.

Mum and I ate that night in a pub near Simonside Terrace. We had been hoping to find some of John Baxter's long-lamented black pudding, but made the mistake of assuming that quaint-looking pubs have quaint clientele and quaint menus. This one served sullen-looking meals from *bains-maries*. We settled for the ubiquitous fish and chips and watched the Friday night crowd assemble around us. Mum spoke about her father's culinary skills: the stuffing Mum always uses for roasts, made simply from bread and herbs, was a recipe she picked up from her dad. My mouth watered as I examined the shell of batter for some remnant of fish.

Ena, our hostess, was right about one thing. The people around us were young. The boys had generally spent their fashion dollars on their heads and feet: impressive boots and impressive ear-rings accentuated by shaved heads. The T-shirts and shabby jeans stretched in between the boots and ear-rings were incidental to the whole effect. Most of the women presented themselves in satin, which was obviously a scarce commodity in Newcastle. They were wearing either pants that scarcely made it around their backsides or dresses that scarcely made it over them.

A band was preparing in the next room. The people at the bar set their jaws in response. It was an audience which liked to experience music as a form of assault. Of all places, this is where Mum got talking about how her parents met. John Baxter had not been long in Australia when he made friends with a fellow engineer, Fred Fearon. Fred had met two presentable young sisters, Agnes and Linda. He arranged for the four of them to go to a home in Drummoyne, a suburb of Sydney, on a double date, although I'm sure during World War I some other terminology would have been used to describe the arrangement. At the end of the outing, Fred asked John which of the two girls he preferred. John had long since learnt to play his cards close to his chest and guessed that Fred wanted to set up a competition. 'I prefer Agnes,' said John, knowing that Fred would then set his cap at Agnes, trying to defeat him in the love game. In fact, John was attracted to Linda. He had steered Fred off his course. Mum told these stories tenderly. She then said how much she loved me.

At this point, one of the young women in tight satin leant across the bar. I was distracted for a moment.

'What did you say, Mum?'

Twenty-one

THAT EVENING, MUM was adamant that we weren't going to start chasing up any information about the Baxters in the Heaton library. She said I didn't know when to leave well enough alone. Next morning, however, she was more amenable to the idea of a little exploration. We went first to the Civic Centre, which was open on Saturday only for weddings. This was where all the satin in Newcastle had got to. The weddings were held in a small parlour inside the front door and followed each other at least every half hour. If a bride, or a groom for that matter, arrived late they could easily find themselves pledging to love and honour the wrong person.

We cut from there to the Newcastle Library, which is a hideous concrete bunker linked by concrete overpasses to a concrete car park on one side and a concrete courtyard on the other. The courtyard was surrounded by three other concrete buildings.

'Cold as charity,' said Mum.

Inside, our spirits dwindled further. There were so many John Baxters in the register of births, deaths and marriages that we could either conclude that Mum was descended from many fathers or give up the case. We decided to content ourselves with a few gimmicks from the souvenir shop. We got a Newcastle pencil sharpener and a Newcastle eraser.

I went into the toilet, where my eye fell on the range of posters on the wall advocating everything from safe sex and condom usage to free contraceptive advice. The full range of human interests. There was also news about confidential HIV counselling and a program called 'positive safe sex'. Amid all this goodwill and community cheer, there was one poster urging people to take a positive attitude to electoral enrolment.

A penny dropped. I went upstairs looking for electoral rolls. I picked out the roll for 1907, the first year in which John Baxter's name could have appeared in the register, being the year after his twenty-first birthday. Sure enough, he was listed at 26 Simonside Terrace. Both Mum and I became excited. We had found something in black and white. Looking back a little, we found John Baxter listed as the ratepayer at that address since 1893. This meant the name in the register was not Mum's father but her grandfather; contrary to what we had thought possible, the eleven children must in fact have grown up in that small tenement. The same John Baxter was paying rates in Simonside Terrace until the end of World War I, by which time Mum's father was half way round the world.

The other thing that comes clear from browsing through the electoral rolls is the growth of Heaton. This should have occurred to me earlier: Heaton is located exactly half way between the uppity end of Newcastle, where our hotel was located, and the end near the port, which comprises mainly working accommodation. The proliferation of those identical houses represented the outbreak of a middle class. In twenty years, Heaton seems to have gone from zip to becoming the densely settled area we had poked around the night before.

A gentleman called Colin noticed us chewing over these hefty tomes and took an interest. He advised us to look at the census from 1891, which was the most recent available to the public. Sure enough, John Baxter, from Scotland, was living at the address with his wife Maggie and, by that stage, five children. The eldest son was John Baxter: within three years he would have taken up smoking. Maggie Clark, we discovered, was born in Toronto in Canada in 1859. Her husband was a 'consulting marine engineer'. On one side lived a 'brewer's agent', also with five children. On the other side was a 'master engine builder'. Our guess about this being an early model of the now familiar middle-class neighbourhood seemed right.

It's hard to explain the way we were moved by such simple contact with the Baxters. We had found some footprints, however faint. Mum said that, on its own, finding the census was worth the trip to England. I felt the same. Mum's earlier reticence had, to some extent, been the fear of disappointment if we found nothing. In an ugly concrete building, leading off an ugly concrete plaza, an unasked question had been answered. The Baxters existed. They had been real people. From their lives could have followed any one of thousands of trajectories. Yet they landed at us.

On the way out of town to Hadrian's Wall, Mum said that she'd wanted to name me Simon John Baxter

McGirr, but Dad wasn't having this at any price. So they changed the name on the cot to 'Simon called Michael'. But Dad still wasn't happy. The John Baxter was cut back to John, which is my middle name. Bearing in mind that Mum had only one sister and that she had four daughters, it's pretty obvious that the last vestige of the long line of John Baxters dies with me. Having no children. This is one edge of the precipice on which I celebrate Mass.

We are waiting. Dad has found what he's looking for. A fountain in a park. He reads the inscription. He comes back to the car. We can get out and have a look now. We have been in the car for ages. We have driven to Parkes, six or seven hours west of Sydney. It is hot. We start splashing the water in the fountain. Dad is angry. He wants us to stand still for photos. My sister has to show what a good reader she is by reading the inscription out loud. It says that the fountain was donated by Mr and Mrs Gregory McGirr in memory of their daughter, Clarinda. It is dated in the twenties, fifty years earlier. Clarinda was our aunt. She died when she was three. We don't understand about having such a young aunt. My grandparents were rocked by her death. They left Parkes not long afterwards, marking the place as they left.

Later, Dad finds the house he used to live in. He knocks on the door. Unannounced. A woman answers. They talk. Not for long. He comes back to the car. He is holding his hat. The woman has told him that he might have lived there once but he doesn't live there now.

Twenty-two

WE WERE IN NEWCASTLE on June 22. On June 27, Mum's wedding anniversary, we returned our tiny Vauxhall to the rental company at Heathrow and caught a plane to Rome, where we joined our bus tour of Italy. The whole trip had been organised around this date. It was the feast of Our Lady of Perpetual Succour.

Our Lady of Perpetual Succour is the name given to one of the best-known images of Mary, the mother of Jesus. The image is an icon; it usually has Greek lettering in the corners. It shows Mary holding the baby Jesus, with archangels looking on approvingly from a distance. Succour means help; the image celebrates the belief that Mary helps you out. To my eyes, the image is rather mannered and even artificial. To Mum, it speaks volumes. Mum and I are both Catholic up to our necks. But in different ways. We are divided by a common creed.

I have never been one of those people whose approach to God has been 'prove it to me'; I tend to say 'show me more'. My faith depends on life becoming more dense, chaotic, inexplicable. It smoulders along the strange line of events that make me me. Mum's crackles. Her faith is more exultant. It leaps over detail in its eagerness to get to the safe harbour of 'trust God' or 'let God' or 'let God work it out'. In a way, this faith serves Mum well because it cheats on the hurt which could easily have undermined the faith of a more self-centred person.

Mum's faith explodes at some powerful one-line powder keg about God working everything out. Mine enjoys the journey.

Mum's faith draws pictures. Mine tells stories.

~

I have to resist the temptation to see the picture of Our Lady of Perpetual Succour as part of the contents of a time capsule from way back when Mum was young. Along with laminex tables, Kelvinator fridges and sixties wedding dresses, these pictures turn up in junk shops all the time.

Religion can create consumer products as much as anything. When I was at uni, I studied Spanish with a skinny guy called Marc. He was the first person I'd met whose clothes weighed more than he did. He wore enough leather to survive a high-speed motorbike smash, but nonetheless he trundled leisurely to class on a rusty bicycle. The leather supported numerous chains and silver studs. Before such accessories were common, he had studs planted in his ears, nose and eyebrows: he'd been pierced so many times that his head whistled when the wind blew. This seemed to give him an advantage affecting the Spanish lisp which our teacher required. We became friends and one day he invited me back to his flat. I expected to be offered a joint, or at least some noxious liquor, but instead he served tea in fine bone china. He showed me some knitting he was working on for his girlfriend. What most intrigued me, however, was that his flat, a couple of rooms over a shop called 'Fetish' in inner Melbourne, was entirely decorated with bits and pieces which had been discarded from churches. He picked them up cheaply at junk shops. He had an altar rail around his bed, a shower curtain made from old vestments, a CD player sitting on a lectern, a set of chalices for drinking from, and so on. He had a tiny desk in front of an enormous pew. He had three broken TV sets, each with one of the stations of the cross in the cabinet.

'I call those my TV stations,' he said.

The only thing used correctly was a thurifer which still smoked incense. He also had a picture of Our Lady of Perpetual Succour, identical to Mum's. I asked him why.

'I don't know,' he said. 'I love kitsch. I can't live without kitsch. I just adore kitsch.'

Mum's picture may not be great art but nor is it kitsch, not to her. There's a difference between an icon and an idol. An idol soaks up meaning like a sponge and hides it somewhere dark; an icon reflects meaning like light. Mum's picture is an icon.

~

Mum has only really lived in two homes. When she and Dad moved into their place, John Baxter had just died and the house at Mowbray Road stood empty. Mum didn't bring much with her. She took some of the furniture which John had made by hand. She took the picture of the Sacred Heart of Jesus which had almost cost Linda her marriage. She took a picture of Our Lady of Perpetual Succour which had hung over her parents' bed and hung it over her own. That picture saw more of Mum's tears than we ever did. Together with her transistor radio, it has been her companion on all the nights the space beside her in the bed has been vacant.

Unlike me, Mum can't understand women who don't adopt their husbands' names when they marry. When Mum married, she readily gave up her involvement in the local branch of the Labor Party, in spite of having been secretary for quite some years and in spite of having been one of the small number of youth delegates whose votes ensured the Sydney Opera House project was adopted as policy. She also gave up her financial autonomy. Dad made the money-decisions for them both. The only place I have ever seen Mum's name written in her own hand as *Maureen Baxter* is on the front of a battered old prayer book full of novenas and devotions to Our Lady of Perpetual Succour. That book has seen plenty of battles. It's the program for the heavyweight title fight Mum has fought with God for over sixty years. As both Maureen Baxter and Maureen McGirr, Mum has struggled to stay within the frame of a picture captioned *Trust God* or *Let God look after it.* Those are the types of slogans which get repeated on tea-towels and wall-hangings to the point of appearing utterly banal. But in this case, they are not. They caption a contest between two strong wills: Mum's and God's. There are not too many people who have what it takes to get into the ring with God. It's easier to bludge off the religious experience of others. Many people out-source their spirituality to shopping centres and cinemas, paying somebody else to do it for them. Mum doesn't do that.

~

As we stepped out of the train station near our hotel in Rome on June 27, Mum picked out one of the few signs we could understand. It was advertising the local lottery.

'That's the kind of miracle I need,' said Mum.

It wasn't the kind she got. We picked our way through traffic, got lost a couple of times and let the noise get the better of our tempers. Finally Mum dug into the cabin bag which had been supplied by our tour company and produced a postcard from the church of St Alphonsus which an eccentric friend had sent her in 1970. Mum had held onto it because the address was on the back and Mum hoped one day to come to Rome. The message which the crazy friend had scribbled was typical of the woman as I remembered her: she was disappointed that the postcard picture did not include the little gift shop at which she'd bought the card. Mum was always asking people on their way to Rome to visit this church and bring her back a card or a medal or get something blessed. It was the church in which you find the original picture of Our Lady of Perpetual Succour.

Mum held the postcard over the map like a compass and, sure enough, we eventually arrived at the church, right on six o'clock when the big Mass for the feast was getting under way. In Mum's eyes, arriving at this moment was as miraculous as having her lucky numbers come up in lotto. The church was crowded. There were lots of nuns and most of the congregation was past its first flush of youth. Mum squeezed in silently at the end of one of the pews and I stood down the back. Mum said nothing. At the end of Mass, a priest blessed the congregation with the original picture of which Mum's was a copy. He needed help to lift it. At the back of the church people put coins into a machine which sold copies of the picture and blessed themselves with those. Mum sat silently. When it was all over, she stood and left quietly. I could tell she had been deeply moved. She had found her friend at home and felt welcome. We crossed the road and had a quiet pizza.

'She never lets you down,' Mum said at last, meaning her friend in the picture.

'Happy anniversary, Mum,' I said.

Twenty-three

THE FOLLOWING DAY we joined our guided tour. The tour director called a roll and everyone was asked to nominate where they had come from. What followed resembled the campaign itinerary of a US presidential election. Texas, New Jersey, Illinois, California, Ohio. We were beginning to get a bit anxious. Oklahoma, Washington, Massachusetts, Florida, Louisiana.

'Isn't this marvellous,' somebody said nearby. She couldn't contain her enthusiasm. Her voice could mercilessly hack away the darkest despair. 'Such a variety. People from *everywhere*.'

If the Romans had realised they were building one of the greatest civilisations in history so that twenty centuries later bus loads of folk from the United States could crawl all over it and take photos, pausing only to get their duty-free scotch on the way out, I'm not sure they would have bothered. They would have put Hadrian's Wall on the other side of the Tiber and called it a day. But the Italians, like the British, have discovered the first law of hospitality. The first law applies equally whether you are borrowing a beach house or, as in these cases, borrowing an entire empire. You don't accept hospitality anywhere unless you want a reciprocal visit.

It's a bit rough, however, when the return visit comes not from the people you owe the favour but from their cousins. The Roman Empire never got as far as the United States, although Roman coins have been found in the backyard of a house in Detroit. It turned out they were left behind by the children of the previous occupants.

'People from everywhere, all getting along together,' said the voice. 'All my new friends.'

There was even someone from Italy. The tour guide. Tony. He wore a checked sports jacket which Mum recognised immediately. Tony's photo, wearing the same jacket, had been in the literature provided by the company.

'That means he must be good,' she said, with authority.

We did the sights of Rome. We did the Colosseum. The building pleased everyone because they had all come from places which had bigger stadiums, even if theirs were not, they were willing to concede, quite as old. Tony explained that the 1960 Olympics were not held here but somewhere else. One member of our group, Sebastian, an Italian-American, was trying to draw a smile from his wife.

'You want?' he asked, indicating the ruins.

She did not respond. He tried his luck on three young women from New Jersey who were also on the tour.

'You want? I buy for you.'

~

Had Mum and Dad made it to Rome in 1959, they might have come across Fellini at work creating *La*

Dolce Vita, which was being shot in the months after they were married. The Colosseum features in the opening gambit of *La Dolce Vita*. The film begins with two helicopters flying low over it. One is trailing a gigantic statue of Christ for delivery to the Vatican. The other contains the main character of the film, the journalist Marcello Rubini, and a photographer. The scene encapsulates the film: it puts tradition and beauty in the background of crassness and opportunism and shows the effect. Fellini said of Rome in 1959, when he was filming, that the city was 'gradually becoming the navel of a world sated with living in a new jazz age, waiting for the third world war, or for a miracle, or for the Martians'.

If Mum and Dad had made it here on their honeymoon, they might well have appeared as two of the 800 extras in the film, because Fellini found many of his performers hanging around the streets of Rome. I'm not sure if Dad could have looked suave on film at a Fellini cocktail party, even using the considerable resources of Mum's cosmetic case.

The photographer in the helicopter in Fellini's film is one of the few characters in the history of cinema whose name has entered practically every language of the world. He is called Paparazzo.

A short stroll from the Colosseum, however, we walked in on an entirely different relationship between an artist and a subject. A shutter opens for less than a second; Michelangelo could chip away on a single project for longer than the average life expectancy of his day. In the church of San Pietro in Vincoli we found as much of the tomb of Pope Julius II as Michelangelo managed to complete. The tomb was originally planned on a colossal scale to stand in St Peter's Basilica, but work was continually interrupted by other little jobs Michelangelo had to do, such as when Julius II asked Michelangelo, if it wasn't too much trouble, would he mind putting a bit of paint on the ceiling of the Sistine Chapel. The project of the tomb dragged on for over forty years. Yet when it began, in 1505, Michelangelo was so assured of his powers that on the trips he made to the quarries in Carrara to check personally the quality of marble he was getting, he thought he could carve a huge effigy in the rock right there in the mountain, as a memorial to himself, so that sailors could see it from out at sea. As time went by he became more skilful and less self-assured.

There have been plenty of biographers of Michelangelo but there's a special magic in the work of his contemporary, Giorgio Vasari. Vasari is in the uncanny position of being able to settle arguments by saying 'according to what I learnt from Michelangelo' and he tells some great stories. One night the Pope sent Vasari around to Michelangelo's place to check on some work. Vasari happened to notice, while he was there, one of the legs of a new figure of Christ that Michelangelo was working on at the time. Michelangelo wasn't happy with the figure, so he deliberately dropped the lantern he was carrying so that the house would be plunged into darkness and Vasari unable to see the work. This appears as yet another example of Michelangelo's *terribilità*, the combination of arrogance and humility that struck something akin to fear into the seven popes he served, not to mention lesser mortals: the arrogant gesture of dropping the lantern was followed by a remark from

Michelangelo to Vasari that 'death was tugging at [his] cape' and that one day 'just like this lantern, my body will fall and the light of life will be extinguished'.

The tomb of Julius II, which Mum and I were now looking at, includes the statue of Moses, a work for which Vasari gives high marks. Most of the people on our tour posed with it. The three young women from New Jersey took turns to hold each other's cameras and to rearrange their hair so that it fell like that of Moses. Then they sat on the rail in front of the statue and put their bags at their sides and leant on them in the way that Moses leans on the tablets with the Commandments, appearing to want to hide them away, almost as if he had stolen them or, more likely, was afraid of them. Then they took off their sandals and stretched out their feet to be as close as possible to those of Moses.

'I'd love to get in there and do polish on his toenails,' said one.

'Get outta here.'

'I'm serious.'

'What colour?'

'Black and purple. Same as what I wear.'

'I think you'd look better in a lighter colour.'

'Get outta here.'

Twenty-four

THE FEAST OF SAINTS Peter and Paul, June 29, is the Pope's feast day. The Pope is regarded as the successor of the Apostles Peter and Paul, who died in Rome. This is why the Pope lives in Rome and not Ermington.

Because of the feast day, we had to wait for the Pope to finish saying Mass before we could enter St Peter's Basilica. It was hot. We'd had some relief earlier when we went underground into the Catacomb of St Domitilla, where the three angels from New Jersey, as Tony had taken to calling them, took turns being photographed in the cavities used by the early Christians to bury their dead.

'Send one back to my boyfriend and tell him I'm dead.'

'Why don't you tell him yourself?'

'Get outta here. He'd never believe me.'

'He believed you when you said you loved him.'

'That's different. He'd see through me if I said I was dead.'

'Somebody should start a hotel down here,' said a voice behind a camcorder. 'It's so cool. You could sleep where they put the bodies. Call it niche marketing.'

~

By the time we resurfaced, a woman named Wendy was struggling with the heat. We had discovered Wendy at breakfast when she sat on our table and began quietly sucking up a fistful of pills. She explained to Mum that all these pills were to prevent migraine. Different ones worked in different circumstances: the red ones if it was cool, the yellow ones when it was wet, and so on. Hart, her husband, cheered her on. He had a long nose, long enough to bring in air from some point safely beyond the polluted wetland of his moustache. Montaigne said that the purpose of a moustache was to store smells. Hart's also made them. Wendy needed so many pills today because she hadn't had the chance to get the weather report because all the channels in her room were in Italian.

'You'd have thought they'd at least have CNN,' she complained bitterly.

The beauty of being a hypochondriac is that, even on those tough days when you're feeling fine, you can re-assure yourself that at least you still have hypochondria. It's better than having nothing. Outside St Peter's, Wendy was complaining again.

'I told you I should have taken the heat pills,' she said. 'I should have taken them before we left our room.'

'I'll see if I can find you some fresh canned juice,' said Hart. 'I'm sure there's some imported juice around. Or some water. They sell water in sealed bottles around the Vatican. If the bottle is sealed, you know it's safe. They might be selling holy water.'

'You put holy water on the outside,' she said, 'you don't drink it.'

'You're allowed to drink it in an emergency.'

'Gandhi drank his own piss,' said Ian, the erudite teenager in the group.

'Well, I'm not Gandhi,' said Wendy. 'And neither is my husband.'

As we waited in line for the Basilica, Wendy explained to Mum that she had a special condition that prevented her from standing in the sun. If the Pope didn't finish Mass soon and let us in, she was going to have a blackout. She announced this like an impending crisis of faith. She borrowed clothes from other people in the group and had soon draped herself in such a way that she did look a bit like Gandhi. Before long she was completely mummified.

'It's so hot in all these clothes,' she complained.

One of the features of a visit to St Peter's is the modesty inspection. This is the kind of examination which most Australians on a visit to Bali would flunk. You aren't allowed to wear shorts or sleeveless garments. No swimming costumes, either, unless they have long legs and sleeves. No singlets.

'What about your right to bare arms?' Ian suggested to Wendy.

The modesty inspection has a point. It keeps out nudists and other undesirables. But it was conducted by young men in Ray Ban sunglasses and dark suits who ran their eyes over visitors as if they were recruiting for a harem. They had slicked back hair and teeth cut for barking and acted like they were auditioning for a Quentin Tarantino movie. A young woman with a fistful of rosary beads, which, to my mind, indicated a certain level of seriousness about her visit, was humiliated in front of people who were allowed to swarm past, talking at the top of their voices, just because they had remembered to bring their golf attire. I'd be more comfortable if the signs warned against coming in with a closed mind or an angry heart.

Tony explained that you could side-step many of the regulations in Italy but the modesty inspection was infallible. Most of us capitulated and people who had loaned clothes to Wendy demurely asked for them back. She surrendered them with poor grace. People started covering their shoulders and legs with spray jackets, towels and blankets.

Once you get inside, however, St Peter's strips you bare.

Mum took a few steps forward into the cavernous gloom and stopped. I looked up into the dome that Michelangelo designed late in his life: he never lived to see it finished. In that moment, hundreds of visitors rushed past.

'What on earth are they trying to prove?' I wasn't sure if Mum was talking about the building or the people rushing past. Officials were still clearing away the cheap plastic stacking chairs which come out for big Masses. They weren't part of the original design. I was distracted by the noise.

'When you think,' said Mum, leaving her sentence unfinished before moving on. I went forward to see the statue of St Peter which, only on this day, wears a triple tiara. Tony was excited about this. He said few Romans had ever seen it. I struggled against the crush of the few thousand who were seeing it today.

'When you think what?' I asked Mum when I found her again.

'I don't know. When you think.'

'What?' I was getting testy with her.

Mum drew in breath to say something important.

'When you think that Jesus had nothing.'

It was a naked response. For seventy years, this building had stood as the physical centre of Mum's religion. This was her pilgrimage to Mecca. Yet her first response was almost revulsion. I wanted to put a brake on her reaction and jolly her along and tell her that Jesus would rather have had this as a monument than the Empire State Building or the Crown Casino. I wanted to remind her of the story that when Michelangelo was appointed to complete the building in 1550 he criticised the work that had been done up till then because, he said, it was so dark and had so many hiding places that it looked like it was built for 'the concealment of outlaws, the counterfeiting of money, getting nuns pregnant and other sordid behaviour'. At least we couldn't see any of that going on. But then my eye fell on markings on the floor which we'd been told to look out for. These markings show how far down the nave of the Basilica other great cathedrals would come if they were put inside St Peter's like Chinese boxes. In a way, those lines epitomise the insecurity that underwrites the need to put up a building like this. They let pilgrims know that however much we may all be children of one God, the Catholics have still got the biggest.

St Peter's is meant to be a focus of unity for Christians around the world. Ironically, it was the decision of Leo X in 1513, while Michelangelo was working on the tomb of his predecessor Julius II, to sell indulgences to raise money for the construction of the Basilica that got on the wick of Martin Luther, among others, and led to anything but unity among Christians. Luther posted his famous theses in 1517. St Peter's is so full of bronze, gold leaf and marble that there isn't a painted surface anywhere inside. Baroque is an architecture of exuberant excess. Sometimes, the excess becomes a form of denial, a disguise. The secret of baroque interiors is that they appear to have no secrets: the ornamentation completely overpowers the architecture. It is amply exemplified by the window that Bernini put in the rear of St Peter's. Bernini's window is framed in alabaster and surrounded by angels. You need to be told that it's a window because the last thing you notice is any movement of light. As windows go, it is exhilarating. It's just that, for me, any sense of the divine completely disappears under the materialism of it all.

~

We had already had an experience of baroque design on the previous day, before we joined the tour, when we visited a church known as 'The Gesu'. This is where St Ignatius, who started the Jesuits, is buried. Oddly enough, Michelangelo was consulted about the design of this building but the early Jesuits, with characteristic modesty, thought they'd try and attract a designer with a *really* big name. So Michelangelo didn't get the job. When we arrived, the interior of the building looked like the insides of a footballer's knee undergoing reconstruction. We manoeuvred ourselves around the scaffolding and then looked upwards, trying to catch a glimpse of the famous baroque ceiling. All we could see was a vast safety net, as though the Jesuits were about to perform on the flying trapeze. No such thrills lay in store: the net was just to stop workers dropping their lunch boxes on the heads of the people saying their prayers below.

We asked how to get into the rooms where St Ignatius had lived, which I had heard were next door. The souvenir seller told us it wouldn't be possible because all the Jesuits were on holidays. Since I was a Jesuit myself, and also on holidays, I thought it would be poor form to complain about this inconvenience. Still, he told us, if we went out into the street and rang the doorbell, there might be somebody to let us in. He told us to use the top doorbell and keep ringing it until something happened. The reason for this was that the top bell was the louder of the two. It made a dreadful noise that echoed around the old building. Eventually it would bring somebody to the door, if only to end the noise. As long as we were prepared to weather a storm of bad temper from a priest whose siesta had been broken, we should be OK.

A young Polish Jesuit came to the door, Robert, and he could not have been more charming or helpful. He didn't speak much English, so, according to the Australian custom, we began talking at him loudly in the belief that a person who can't understand a language when spoken at 70 decibels, will become competent in it at 90 decibels and a professor of it at 110.

The approach to the rooms of St Ignatius, like his tomb, is ornate. About one hundred years after he died, there was so much enthusiasm for him that some well-intentioned interior designers turned the corridor leading to his suite into something like the barrel of a kaleidoscope. The walls are painted to look like the cheapest kind of multi-coloured tattoo, the kind that can only be appreciated from the vantage point of a lover.

Luckily, the rooms in which Ignatius spent the nine years of his life before he died in 1556 have been pared back to their original state, as he knew them. The simplicity is refreshing. After the gaudiness of the church and the technicolour corridor, it was pleasant to sit here a while and let the mind wander. Mum told Robert that she didn't have much time for poor old Ignatius.

'You can say what you like,' she said, 'but he was never a mother.'

There is little in the rooms except a few pieces of furniture from Ignatius' period, a few of the clothes he wore and a metal bust on a concrete stand which gives the impression of his exact height – which happened to be the same as Mum's. They could have eyeballed each other. I thought of the stories of Ignatius going onto the roof of this building to look at the stars and making a gesture of reverence under the canopy of creation. The stars were his ceiling.

~

'When you think that Jesus had nothing,' Mum repeated inside St Peter's the following day. I had to concede that it is a mystery how a religion which has as its core experience the humiliating death of a lonely man on a cross can have St Peter's as its central building. But it's hardly relevant to wonder what Jesus would have made of all this because I doubt if Jesus would have made it past the boys in Ray Bans on the steps. There is one unforgettable image of Jesus in St Peter's. That is Michelangelo's

Pieta. Jesus is all but naked in that particular representation; his mother, in contrast, is buried alive in clothing.
It's the only place in the whole disaster where stone
looks like flesh, where you might look to find this entire
pile, complete with endless plastic stacking chairs and
men collecting money, convulse back into life, where
you might notice a ripple of energy across a solid surface. It is, of course, an image of a dead man with his
mother. His body does not appear physically damaged in
any way. I watched it for some time, wondering if these
stones will ever breathe.

Neither Ignatius nor Michelangelo knew their mothers. Michelangelo carved the *Pieta* in St Peter's as a young
man. Vasari says of it that *clearly it is a miracle that a
stone, formless in the beginning, could ever have been
brought to the state of perfection which Nature habitu-
ally struggles to create in the flesh.* He goes on to tell the
story of Michelangelo overhearing the conversation of
some pilgrims in front of the statue who assumed it was
the work of someone else. So he returned under cover of
dark to carve his name into it. He didn't put it on a hem
or on the base of the pedestal. He carved his name across
the mother's breasts. The place he felt absent from. Fifty
years later, Michelangelo created another *Pieta.* In this
one, he included not just his name, but made the figure
of Nicodemus, standing behind Jesus and Mary, a portrait of himself. Nicodemus is not looking at Jesus being
taken down from the cross. He is looking at the mother.

~

That night, we were taken out of town to a wonderful
open-air bistro in the countryside. The colour of the sky

was rich and subtle. You could never hope to match a lipstick to it. There was wine and song and the unsurprising revelation that, once they got into a really good mood, most of our companions chose to relax by telling you all about themselves. It was their hobby.

The woman who was making many friends had suddenly left the tour without explanation. Jodie and Rae had taken her place. They hadn't even known they were coming until a few days before. They had been given the trip by their boss as a reward for their performance at work.

'So you're actors, then,' laughed the voice behind the camcorder.

'You know, we don't even like our boss that much,' said Jodie, ignoring the voice.

'I hope she doesn't expect us to like her just because she's paid for our vacation,' added Rae.

'We've already got her present.'

'What did you get?' asked Mum.

'Nothing.'

Mum laughed and a friendship was formed. She often told us as kids, when our birthdays were coming up, that we were going to get a 'good, big nothing'.

Some of Jodie's luggage had gone missing *en route*.

'I hope not the bag with nothing in it,' said Mum.

We got to talking about our jobs. Jodie and Rae worked for a recruitment agency in California with clients from the entertainment industry. They saw a slice of life. Rae had us in stitches. She said that she knew to expect the worst whenever she rang up a client to offer them casual work and they said 'Well, you see, the thing is.' Before she left, there was one who said she couldn't work: 'The thing is I have to feed my grandmother's goldfish.' The client needed the whole day to do it. There was another one who said, 'The thing is', and went on to explain that it was the last day on which she could have an abortion so she had decided to get on with that instead. She was as matter-of-fact as if it was the last day to buy a lottery ticket. Then she rang back and said that she had spoken to the clinic and she could have the abortion tomorrow so she was happy to work today. It was worth meeting a couple of Californians who appreciated the fact that they were on vacation from insanity. The group rolled home to try and find CNN on TV, hoping for reassurance that the worlds they had left for a moment were still in chaos without them. They had brought their own insanity with them.

Twenty-five

NEXT MORNING, most of us were hung over. Wendy appeared at breakfast looking uncomfortably happy. She was on her own.

'I'm heartless,' she said.

This was Wendy's joke.

'I'm without Hart.'

Her one joke.

Hart appeared, scratching his moustache, which was unusually dry. He grabbed a glass of milk and watered the crop beneath his nose. Then he, too, was happy.

'You two look happy,' said Mum.

'Oh,' said Wendy, suddenly disappointed, 'do we?'

'I'm afraid so,' said Mum, justified in her opinion by the small number of pills Wendy had brought to breakfast. Wendy was not going to rack up too many frequent fever points today.

We rotated seats and got to meet new people. We couldn't avoid it. The man across from us shot out his hand.

'Hi,' he said. 'I'm Max.'

'Pleased to meet you,' said Mum, looking anything but pleased.

'And this is Min.'

A small woman pulled her face out of her carry-on bag and smiled.

'We're on the news every night,' said Max.

'Oh, you managed to find CNN.'

'No. We don't watch the news. We're on the news.'

'Max and Min,' prompted Min. 'Get it?'

'Max temperature for today. Min temperature for today,' added Max.

'On the weather,' continued Min.

'Max the dollar reached. Min the dollar fell today.'

'On the finance.'

'Max life expectancy.'

'Min risk.'

'We're famous.'

~

We were moving by 7 a.m. to get to the Sistine Chapel early. Even at that hour, the line to get in stretched around the block. It made you think how easily an army of tourists could completely besiege the Vatican. I presumed the Pope must have taken a turn for the worse and the mad rush was to get in and have a look before a conclave started in the Chapel. Once the Cardinals gather in the Sistine Chapel to begin voting for a new Pope, tourist visits are limited.

The real reason for our hurry was that the last Sunday of the month you can get into the Vatican museum, and hence the Sistine Chapel, free of charge. This meant there was going to be a big crowd. We got there over an hour before opening.

'At least you can add the Sistine Chapel to your list,' I said to Mum.

'What list?'

'The list of things you got for free.'

Standing in line, we could hear Max and Min having a life and death discussion. From time to time, they broke into jovial banter, especially when others were milling around. They told us they came from St Petersburg.

'But that don't make me a Ruskie.'

St Petersburg, Illinois. There is a city in Russia named after it, Min conceded, but its only claim to fame is that it provided a backdrop for *Dr Zhivago*.

'Max in summer, one hundred and ten.'

'Min in winter, ten.'

It was becoming clear, however, that beneath their well-oiled routine they were both anxious about finding a drink. They must already have worked their way through what they'd picked up at the duty-free shop. They needed a 'heart-starter' and wanted to know if there were any bars nearby where they could pop in for a 'quick one'. They used the old familiar technique of wondering things out loud in the hope that they would be overheard and therefore not have to ask the question themselves.

'Max ten minutes.'

'Min delay.'

Tony didn't seem able to help.

'Oscar Wilde said he drank to keep body and soul apart,' said Max. 'But occasionally we need a little something to keep Max and Min together.' Like many before them, they didn't think they could face the Sistine Chapel without at least one stiff drink. Before long, they were wondering aloud whether it would be worth missing the Chapel altogether so they could have a drink and feel more relaxed for the rest of the day.

'We've seen it on TV,' said Min.

'It's like going to the Superbowl. You see more if you stay at home and watch it on TV.'

'They should have a TV on the bus for people who don't want to get off and some videos of the major attractions.'

~

We spent far longer in the line for the Sistine Chapel than we did in the Chapel itself. People were at a loss to know how to fill in the time. Mum started making up stories about passers-by. Jodie and Rae laughed.

'Your mother is so cooool.'

Twenty-six

PEOPLE DO NOT CREATE stories as a luxury. They do it to survive. Take *The Thousand and One Nights*.

The summer Dad first got sick, Mum made up a lot of stories.

Dad was skinny when he married. As a rake. We have photos of him and Mum on Mum's other honeymoon, the one that lasted four days. They went to a wildlife sanctuary in Brisbane. Dad gave Mum a koala to hold against her beautiful new travelling suit; Dad wrapped a snake around his neck and pointed its fangs at the camera. He liked the photos so much that he paid extra to have them made from black-and-white into colour. He cut the end off his tie so the reproduction artist could match the colours accurately.

Thirteen years later, when he returned to Brisbane with three children in tow, he had gained twenty-five kilograms. We booked a bus tour that took us north from Sydney along the coast. Mum was carsick the whole way; she sat stoically over an air vent in the bus and wished she was back at home. When we got to Surfers Paradise, we found that Mum and Dad had not thought to bring anyone's swimming costumes. So we all climbed into the hotel pool in our underpants. Other than that, we spent most of the time in a small European cafe we had discovered at the end of a dark arcade.

It was called 'The Blue Danube' and had maroon carpet and thick velvet wallpaper. We were the first customers each day; our arrival was marked by the proprietor putting a scratchy vinyl record of Strauss waltzes on the turntable and asking Dad if he wanted his steak well done again today. And his waffles with extra golden syrup. And butter. After lunch, which was normally over by 11.30 a.m., we went ten pin bowling. This was Dad's favourite sport. Mum helped him put on his shoes, because he had trouble reaching over his belly. It was a curious way to spend time at a surfing resort. In Brisbane itself, we stayed in Lennons Hotel, where Mum and Dad had spent their first night as a couple. Dad complained that the plumbing was even noisier than it had been all those years before. He and Mum were weary of travel already, so we paid extra to turn our bus tickets into air tickets and flew home immediately. Dad was unable to put the meal table down in front of him in the plane.

Three years later when we went on our next bus tour, to visit Dad's sisters in Melbourne, Dad weighed less than when he had got married.

~

After we'd got back from the Brisbane trip, our orthodontist noticed that I had a tied tongue, meaning it was anchored by an unnecessary piece of skin to the floor of my mouth and couldn't move properly. It was odd that nobody had noticed such an obvious explanation for the fact that I had some problems with speech and, more significant to young Michael, that I couldn't whistle properly. Every time I tried to whistle, I could only produce a fine spray of spittle. Sometimes it wasn't even so fine. I went into hospital a day or two after Christmas.

When I returned from under the anaesthetic, my mother and sister were at my bedside. Their faces looked blurred, as though they were under water. I surfaced slowly. Finally I could see them clearly. They waited patiently for hours, until I was feeling more like myself. Then they started telling funny, made-up stories about the people in the other beds.

'I have to take your father to a specialist,' said Mum after a few stories.

I heard but could not speak. My mouth was sore and numb.

'He's got sick. The doctor doesn't know what's wrong. He wants him to see somebody else.'

Dad had been off colour for a few weeks, but we assumed it was a cold or a flu. For days on end, while ordinary people were on holidays, Mum and we three kids sat in the car while Dad was moved from doctor to doctor. Most of them had rooms in slender buildings in Sydney's Macquarie Street. There were so many narrow buildings in the street that it looked like they were holding their breath so they could all fit in. It was hard to find a place to park in Macquarie Street. As well as the truck, Dad had by now bought a ten-year-old Holden which we called 'the pink lady' because of its garish colour. This was the same car which was bequeathed to my brother and which I managed to write off. It had plastic vinyl seats which sweated in the heat. So Mum had to contend with cranky kids, menacing parking officers and increasing uncertainty about Dad's health. It was clear he was suffering from more than a cold.

Mum relieved the pressure by making up stories about the people who were coming and going from the office blocks nearby:

'See that woman. She's waiting for her boyfriend.'

'How do you know?'

'I just know. The boyfriend's late, you see. That's why she looks so bad-tempered.'

We stopped brawling in the back long enough to look at the woman's face. The story was plausible.

'The boyfriend might be seeing another woman.'

We were fighting again.

'Look. Here he comes.'

We sat up. The man Mum was talking about walked right past the woman.

'No. Not him. It might be this one.'

Sure enough, the woman's face beamed when she saw the next man Mum had nominated, and she kissed him.

'I don't know about that,' said Mum. 'She's trying to make him feel that he's the ant's pants.'

Mum taught us how to look for clues. Shoes were important in her detective work. If a young man had dirty shoes, it meant he was taking his girlfriend for granted. If an older man had clean shoes, it meant he was taking his wife for granted because, in all likelihood, she was the one who was cleaning them. If a man had elasticised boots under the trousers of his suit, it meant he didn't wear the suit often and was therefore seeing somebody as a client. If a man wore business shoes under jeans, it meant he didn't wear the jeans often and was having a day off.

Dad returns to the car. He gets in.

'More tests.'

He takes off his hat and holds it between his hands like he does in church.

'They don't tell you much,' he concludes.

Twenty-seven

WE WAITED WHILE Dad went to another appointment. Mum told us about umbrellas. People with the transparent plastic umbrellas which came right down over your head and which were trendy in the seventies could be going to meet somebody special, because those umbrellas forced a couple to walk shoulder to shoulder, if not arm in arm. People with folding umbrellas were on their own because they were so small and, besides, the wind turned them inside out easily, so that you wouldn't risk looking like a fool in front of somebody you were keen to impress. Big umbrellas meant you were keeping the world at arm's length. We were lucky it rained so much in the hot Sydney summer. Otherwise we would never have learnt all this.

We had to speculate about what magazines people in the street were likely to pick up from the news-stand opposite. We had to assess the character of the strangers by their appearance. It wasn't too hard when young women picked up *Cleo* or when men in overalls picked up *Best Bets*. But when a woman picked up *Modern Motor*, we had to come up with an explanation.

'Maybe she's buying it for her father.'

'More likely to get in good with her boss,' suggested Mum, always enriching the story with a conspiratorial edge. Then we had to invent silly names for magazines.

'What about *Horse and Garden?*'

'*Neapolitan?*'

'*Oldsweek?*'

We were only kids.

'The *Cowetin?*'

Dad reappears. He doesn't look as if he'd like playing word games.

He sits in the passenger seat beside Mum and untangles the seat belt which the law has forced him to have installed, much against his wishes. He fits the buckle. This is our place for confidences. For a moment my brother, my sister and I don't exist. He turns to Mum like she's the only one in the car.

'Kidney trouble,' he says.

Two words. We all know them. Mum's only sister died of kidney trouble a few years ago. The same story runs through all our minds without any of us needing to say a word.

'Home?' asks Mum

'Sydney Hospital,' says Dad. 'They're expecting me.'

Twenty-eight

WHEN WE GOT TO Ward 17, the nursing staff were amazed to see Dad walk through the door. The level of toxins in his body was so high that the doctor had wanted to call an intensive care ambulance. But Dad was making this trip in the front of the car. Dad's kidneys had taken a battering from the APCs on which he had become dependent. Once they started to malfunction, he took more and more APCs to alleviate the symptoms of pain he was getting. He had been caught in a rapid downward spiral.

At the hospital, we sat and read every magazine in the waiting room while, unknown to us, the staff worked out how long Dad could possibly survive. They gave him thirty-six hours.

Mum went into practical mode. There were things that needed to be done, relatives that needed to be rung, health insurance that needed to be checked. Late that night she took us home and got us something to eat. Then she went into her room alone and poured it all out to the picture of Our Lady of Perpetual Succour. She went to sleep with the radio playing talkback all night.

Next day, she went up the street and bought a small green overnight bag for the few things that Dad would need in hospital.

'That old Gladstone bag has had it,' she said. 'I'm sick to death of trying to get it open. Besides, he'll need this one for a long time.'

Getting the bag was her vote of confidence in the future.

Twenty-nine

IN THE CRUSH for the Sistine Chapel, you will notice every conceivable genus and species of nun. Budding clothes designers should go there just to see how many different things you can do with a veil. The only thing they seemed to have in common was that they all carried make-up compacts. None of the nuns made any attempt to conceal them.

The door to the Chapel is tiny and takes you through a wall so thick that for a moment you feel like you're in a tunnel – a reminder that the Chapel was built to be heavily fortified. It was only on finally getting inside, about four hours after we'd been roused from sleep, that I realised what all the nuns' compacts were for. They'd been brought for their mirrors. The nuns held them down, at arm's length, so they could look at the ceiling without craning their necks or dislodging their veils. Here were hundreds of nuns, under one of the most famous ceilings in the world, and they seemed to want to look at nothing other than the floor.

Mum was suitably impressed with Michelangelo's ceiling. After all, she had painted every square inch of the ornate ceilings she had at home, so she spoke with authority. Indeed, Michelangelo never had to contend with three young children trying to come up the ladder after him or suck the paint off his brushes.

Nor did Michelangelo ever have to repaint the entire duco on his partner's truck. By the seventies the truck in which Dad collected Mum on their first date had started to look a bit sorry. Dad wasn't at all sure what to do. He was worried that it would be declared unroadworthy. So Mum painted the whole thing bright peppermint green, which was a trendy colour at the time for small imported vehicles. She then stencilled *Greg McGirr, North Sydney* under the driver's door. Painting the 'old bus' was a labour of love. You wouldn't do it for any other reason.

Michelangelo didn't just paint for love:

I, Michelangelo, sculptor, have this day received from His Holiness our Lord Pope Julius II, five hundred papal ducats . . . on account of the painting of the vault of the chapel of Pope Sixtus, regarding which today I am starting work.

That was in 1508. The work required extraordinary physical efforts. Michelangelo had to devise a working platform which concealed the ceiling from onlookers on the ground and yet provided enough light to work by. This scaffolding projected out from the wall. The artist had to lean at vertiginous angles. The artificial light created uncomfortable heat. Dust made breathing difficult. In 1510, Michelangelo wrote a poem to a friend about the experience: *I live in hell and paint its pictures.*

The ceiling is a highly physical painting. The figures on the ceiling seem on the one hand to be boxed in and on the other hand breaking free from their confinement. It is a restless work. God may be calm but the energy in the entire thing is anything but. The painting is a boiling cauldron in which only God the Father experiences a still moment. Yeats wrote:

> There on that scaffolding reclines
> Michael Angelo.
> With no more sound than the mice make
> His hand moves to and fro.
> Like a long-legged fly upon the stream
> His mind moves upon silence.

Michelangelo started work on the ceiling when he was thirty-three and finished when he was thirty-seven. Twenty-five years later, he returned to do the work which occupies the entire back wall of the chapel. This painting is called *The Last Judgement*. By the time Michelangelo got to it, Rome had been invaded and many of the Renaissance ideals were starting to look a bit shabby. In contrast to the ceiling, most of the figures on the back wall are static. They have reached their final destination. It is an enthralling and frightening work. The word has become a cliché, but this *is* also a subversive work, especially given its location – bold enough to consign one prominent contemporary cleric, Biagio da Cesena, to the underworld. Biagio had complained about having nudes in a place of worship. Michelangelo retaliated by using him as the model for the satanic figure of Minos. When Biagio asked the Pope to intervene, the Pope told him that he could have helped if Biagio was shown in purgatory, but there was no hope of getting him out of hell.

Michelangelo had included a self-portrait in his earlier work. In the corner of the ceiling is a representation of one of the less savoury biblical stories, that of Judith beheading Holofernes. The face on the head on the platter is that of the artist. *The Last Judgement* incorporates an entirely different self-portrait. Michelangelo's vision of the world had grown darker in twenty-five years, even become embittered. In the middle of the *Judgement*, on the skin of St Bartholomew, is a portrait of the artist, a portrait that struggles to keep its shape. It's as though in the great mass of humanity in that painting, Michelangelo couldn't work out where he fitted himself in. He is suspended between heaven and hell. You can't tell if he is going to sink or swim. Beneath him are swarms of the damned.

When the chapel is crowded, it is difficult to tell where this painting begins and ends. The forlorn figures in the bottom of the picture extend seamlessly into the crush of tourists. Michelangelo lures you into the space then condemns you for being there. Meanwhile, guards are barking at anybody who looks like they are about to pull out a camera, and a recorded message asks over and over in three languages for silence. You can hardly hear the message over the din.

Michelangelo was sixty-six when he finished *The Last Judgement*. He had seriously injured himself when he fell from the scaffold in the course of his work. The Sistine Chapel has a little of that effect on everyone. It's like a time machine. You can feel yourself ageing as you

stand there, buffeted by the crowds, assaulted by the
paintings. Michelangelo told stories to survive. In a
world which had turned pageantry into banality, he
could turn the commonplace into drama.

On our way out, we met Wendy sitting with hunched
shoulders and holding her head. She had a migraine.

'She must have taken the wrong pills,' explained Hart.

Thirty

NEXT WE HEADED for Ostia, the ancient sea port for Rome. Its quietness was a welcome relief. In *La Dolce Vita*, Ostia is the place you escape to when you're escaping from escapism and want to give your sports cars a bit of an outing. But it has a much longer history than that. Twenty centuries ago, trade between Ostia and North Africa was so intense that goods sealed in barrels could be imported to Italy within three days of their despatch from Africa. I doubt if service could be any better these days. Unfortunately, constant flooding caused the city to be abandoned and it was eventually covered with silt, only to be rediscovered at the end of the nineteenth century. As a result, the whole metropolis is reasonably preserved, complete with baths, amphitheatres, forum and bars. It doesn't take much imagination to think that the people have just walked out, Ostia had a population of about 100 000, so they must have lived at close quarters. Indeed, quarters don't come much closer than the public ablutions block, a structure which particularly tickled the interest of the three young women from New Jersey, who began speculating about who, if they had to share a seat in the lavatory, they would prefer to share it with.

'Over the pit with Brad Pitt.'

'Get outta here.'

They were even more enthusiastic about the entire street of bars, where you can imagine Ostia starting to hum in the middle of the night. The local guide had no difficulty decoding the strange ways of New Jerseyan enthusiasm, in which a positive reaction is expressed as a negative and vice versa.

'If you step into this room where I am now, you can see some original mosaics,' said the guide.

'Get outta here.'

'If you stand on the nodal point of the amphitheatre you can be heard at the back without raising your voice.'

'Shut up.'

'Get outta here' was an affirmation. 'Shut up' was, it seemed, a positive term of endearment.

'I hope you have enjoyed your tour of Ostia.'

'Get outta here and shut up.'

The guide was beaming.

Ancient Ostia wasn't just a close-packed settlement of shysters, hucksters and guild members, however; not everyone carved their reputation with a dagger or had somebody else resolve their conflicts in narrow back lanes. Among all the chaos of that place and time, there was room for a different type of personality. This was also the home of Monica, the mother of St Augustine. Augustine is famous for his wayward youth and is said to have made the prayer, 'Lord give me chastity but not yet.' He was the father of a boy called Adeodatus. His mother is famous for praying for his conversion. Her prayers were answered and one of Augustine's first steps when he mended his ways was to send his concubine packing, in spite of the fact she had stood by him for twelve years. This has struck many observers as rough justice.

Augustine didn't stop there; his legacy sent concubines packing throughout the Christian world. And not just concubines. Much of the Christian hostility to the human body which has caused psychological damage over the years, rightly or wrongly, is now traced to Augustine. Augustine is made responsible for a stiffness and inflexibility which a friend of mine, with a weakness, calls 'Ostia-porosis'. Augustine was a phenomenal intellect and wrote more books than most people read in a lifetime. He nutted out some important problems implied by the Christian world view. He thought long and hard about what should be salvaged when an entire culture is vulnerable to destruction. There is no doubt that the world would have been poorer had he decided to live with his mother, get some tattoos and work on the dock. But he disembodied himself. This was a crying shame.

There is a scene in his *Confessions*, shortly before Monica's death, where Augustine is visiting her in Ostia. They are looking out a window together, into a garden, when they start wondering what eternal life might be like:

> *Our conversation led us to the conclusion that no bodily pleasure, however great it might be and whatever earthly light might shed lustre upon it, was worthy of comparison, or even of mention, beside the happiness of the life of the saints.*

Sex and grief are deeply intermeshed. I went through my Augustine period at the same time I was going through my AC/DC period: when I realised that Dad was living on borrowed time. I wasn't prepared to think about death until I had The Answer. And a kid with precocious answers is trying to take a short cut through adolescence. It doesn't work.

St Monica lived in the port which linked Europe to the parts of North Africa over which her inscrutable son became the Bishop. In Ostia, there is a plaque quoting words from Augustine's *Confessions* about her:

> *She had talked in a motherly way to some of my friends and had spoken to them of the contempt of this life and the blessings of death . . . and so on the ninth day of her illness, when she was fifty-six and I was thirty-three, her pious and devoted soul was set free from the body . . . She had not died in misery, nor had she wholly died.*

Augustine keeps his grief snap-frozen in the same way he chills his sexuality. He kicks himself for crying: it reminds him that he hasn't put enough faith in God. This looks suspiciously like denial. It's hard nowadays to think of death as the welcome moment at which the soul is set free from the body. The body is not a prison. It's not meant to be, although people who spend their lives worrying about how they look turn it into one. The body is your home, the home you grow up in. Eventually you have to leave it. I can tell you from experience that leaving home isn't so easy. It doesn't matter how much faith you have, death ain't easy either.

Thirty-one

WE WOUND THROUGH the fields of Tuscany, stopping for a Chianti tasting in one of the villas. More than a tasting, to be honest. The group became so merry that, instead of coming up the front of the bus to unburden their life story through the microphone, people started coming up to tell jokes. The life stories were funnier. It was a little unnerving to have your first taste of Tuscany as part of a rolling audition for the David Letterman show. Eventually, I was called to take my turn so I lurched forwards to the front, hoping to be able to keep a fair taste of Chianti below the water line as I did so. I don't have much repertoire of jokes, but made up one about a rooster and a camel.

I was succeeded by young Ian, who squeezed a pimple into the rear-vision mirror of the bus before taking the microphone. He told the group that Dieresis and Ellipsis were the Roman gods of punctuation. I wished I'd thought of that.

~

There are worse places than Florence. It must be one of the few cities in the world where a guide can point casually to the place where Michelangelo and Leonardo had a blue in the street. This is one incident which Vasari passes over. He merely reports there was a great animosity between the two, as a result of which Michelangelo left town. The story goes that Leonardo and a few mates were passing the time in the square. In Renaissance Florence you didn't stand around talking football. The blokes were discussing the poet Dante. Leonardo happened to notice Michelangelo walking past and told his mates that Michelangelo could explain the verses that were troubling them. Michelangelo must have hit his thumb with a hammer that morning because, thinking he'd been slighted, he turned on Leonardo and accused him of not finishing work he started, which, as a final insult, does sound like the pot calling the kettle black. If Michelangelo then threatened to put a moustache on the face of the *Mona Lisa*, Vasari fails to mention it.

Michelangelo and Leonardo tend to be contrasted rather than compared but they share a least two things in common, apart from having kept drink-coaster designers and calendar makers in business for generations. The first is that, like Ignatius, they were brought up by men. The second is that, as adults, they had big problems getting close to people.

Leonardo was older than Michelangelo. He was on a committee which had to decide where to put the enormous statue of David which Michelangelo completed in 1504. Most of Florence turned out to see the statue being shifted. In one of his asides, Vasari lets us know that he still has the drawings for the special slip-knots Michelangelo invented so the statue could be moved.

Shifting the 'Giant', as it came to be called, was a bit like shifting the Statue of Liberty in one piece. David is huge. It makes you wonder what Goliath would have looked like if Michelangelo had wanted to make the companion piece.

The statue was left out of doors until the end of the nineteenth century, when it was put inside out of the weather and away from vandalism. In 1512, for example, one of its arms was broken during a siege. Vasari, who just happened to be standing nearby, picked up the pieces and took them home. I'm jealous of Vasari. He must have had a lot of great stuff in his house. It comes as no surprise to discover that he was the architect for the famous Uffizi Gallery: he was used to housing priceless works of art. He had a garage full of them. This is why the Uffizi feels so much like a Renaissance warehouse.

~

I picked a stone off the street and tried to convince Mum that it was an undiscovered Michelangelo miniature.

'For God's sake, put that down and find somewhere to wash your hands.'

Obediently, I left Mum to hold my place in the queue. Unfortunately, Florence does not share with Paris that handy invention known as 'the can-can': a self-cleaning metal cylinder, equipped with lavatory, where you pay a couple of francs for your privacy. This allows a fifteen-minute parking limit before the door swings open on you. This explains why an especially energetic dance is named after the device. All I could find in Florence was a phone box, outside the

Accademia. I decided to phone the office in Melbourne to see if they remembered who I was.

'Oh, hi, Mick.'

'How's things?'

'Fine.'

'I mean, how are things without me?'

'Just fine. We've sent the magazine to press and all went well.'

This was dreadful news.

'And there were no hiccups without me?'

'None at all. Do you want to talk to anyone in particular?'

My colleagues had the temerity to be surviving without me.

'I'm just ringing in to see if you need to run anything past me?'

'No. Nothing. You just enjoy yourself.'

The temerity to be doing well without me.

'Everyone sends their love and we all want you to have a great time.'

And the insensitivity to let me know.

This disappointing conversation cost me twelve bucks. Perhaps it was being at a slightly lower ebb than usual which made me more aware of some of the illegal immigrants hanging around the line outside the Accademia. People with nowhere to phone. If only because my ego had been slightly bruised, I felt some momentary fellow feeling with the *sans-papiers* who bob up all over Europe. Most of them appeared to have come from Africa. They were trying to sell posters. The posters were mostly either religious kitsch or smutty kitsch, proving again that religion and smut both sell, but not always to the same folk. Such impresarios are not new on the scene; Charles Dickens caught them out of the corner of his eye when he was in Italy in 1845.

Dickens' accounts of his travels are worth reading because he coincided with the birth of mass tourism, the package tour and fast food; his tone conveys the first traces of the weary cynicism and strained humour which has become the stock in trade of contemporary travel writing. He marvels that you can get from Rome to London in eight or nine days, a journey which was once considered as taking Roman soldiers 'beyond the limits of the world'. God knows what Dickens would have thought of putting a Visa card in a box and speaking to the land to which Micawber disappeared and from which Magwitch turned up. But Dickens had an eye to people left behind in the rush. He says that Pisa might be considered the seventh wonder of the world because of its architecture, but it's really the second wonder of the world because of the number of beggars there.

The beggars seem to embody all the trade and enterprise of Pisa. Nothing else is stirring except warm air.

Their successors are still working the line outside the Accademia. Outside the Uffizi and the Louvre. Outside every museum and gallery. Outside.

Thirty-two

IN THE EVENING we were taken to a vantage point where we could look back over Florence. Dozens of refugees and vagrants were bedding down in the dusk. In spite of this, Jodie was feeling romantic. She told Ian – the teenager whose parents were using the tour to demonstrate how much they disliked each other – that he should come back here for his wedding. Ian looked at her like she was stupid.

'Well, I wouldn't mind getting married here,' Jodie said to Mum.

'I could think of better things to do with my time,' said Mum, fanning herself in the heat.

Jodie laughed.

'Your mother is so cooool.'

We went on to another bistro, a converted farmhouse on the outskirts. It's never a good omen to arrive at a restaurant and find a fire engine in the drive. Indeed, we could see smoke billowing from the kitchen. Undaunted, the head waiter told us that the only problem was that twenty litres of fat had caught fire on the stove. As Hart translated the waiter's perfect English into intelligible

American we learnt there'd be no problem fixing us a feed. In the meantime, we were asked to go into the garden.

'Get outta here.'

'Max inconvenience.'

But, we were assured, free beverages would be served.

'Min problem.'

'Max appreciation.'

We had time, sitting under the trees, to discuss the real treasures of Florence – its shopping. Sebastian had bought every member of his family a leather jacket. Wendy had wanted to try one on, but the air conditioning in the shop wasn't cool enough for her to risk it. Jodie said she wasn't a leather girl. The girls from New Jersey said they weren't either, but a bargain was a bargain. Tess, Ian's mother, said she certainly was a leather girl but she wasn't going to give her nearly-ex husband the pleasure of seeing her in leather. Connie, a Jewish lady from Texas, had bought a ten-gallon handbag.

Leigh – the woman who had stood at the front of the bus to announce that she had divorced her husband so they could put some spice into their lives by living together in sin – had been through a traumatic experience earlier in the day when she had come down to breakfast and found Wendy wearing an identical dress to hers. She knew she ought not have brought chain-store clothes to tour the unique wonders of Italy. Furthermore, the experience had reactivated a childhood trauma when she had turned up to one of her school proms wearing the same dress as another girl.

But then she started explaining to Mum that she had had her own Michelangelo experience as well. She was a creative person and did paintings.

'Tell us about the Michelangelo experience,' said the voice behind the camcorder.

Leigh became more confident once she was talking to a camera.

We gathered that a 'Michelangelo experience' was an experience of being intuitive. Leigh attached a great value to intuition. She said her dreams were highly intuitive. She envied a friend who had kept a dream diary for years. She could go back and read about dreams she had had twenty or thirty years before. Leigh said that her dreams were her prayers.

'Tell us about the Michelangelo experience,' said Mum. She wasn't going to miss out on a good story

Reluctantly, Leigh got to the point. Another friend of hers, an animal lover, once got four new dogs and, before she'd even seen them, Leigh decided to do a painting of them as a Christmas present for her friend. She wanted to capture the personality of each dog.

'You know how busy you are on Christmas? Well, she rang me right up on Christmas morning. She said, "Leigh, those dogs are perfect." I hadn't even seen them, yet she said the dogs were perfect.'

That was her Michelangelo experience. She had painted perfect dogs, sight unseen.

Soon we knew that most of the people at the table saw psychics, at $100 an hour. One had taken this trip because she read about it in her horoscope. If you have anything to sell the best thing to do is to write a horoscope directing people to your business. Jodie's sister worked as a psychologist specialising in relationships between mothers and daughters. She had moved into this area of specialty on account of the humiliation she had suffered at the hands of her own mother. This was a cue to batten down for a horror story. It was a horror story. Horrific in its banality. Their mother had taught Jodie's sister to ski when she was thirteen. She resented the fact that she had been made to stand on skis when she was at her most awkward stage of development. Her grievance was so deep that she had been able to mine it for an entire career.

~

We all got merry once more. Back at the hotel, Mum went off to bed while Jodie and Rae invited me into the bar. We got talking. Bill, who was doing the tour with his father and sister, joined us. Bill's dad had emigrated to the United States as a young man: this was his first visit back in forty-three years. Before joining the tour, they had gone to his old village where his father was overjoyed when some of the old folk recognised him.

'It meant the world to him.'

It meant the world to have one tiny piece of the world to call his own. Bill was an engineer. His father had told him that you can't build a village like the one he came from with a ruler and pencil. Bill answered that, in that case, it was no wonder they couldn't find anywhere to park. But there was another side of Bill. He conducted white-water rafting tours 'back home' and was contemptuous of customers who wanted a real experience without getting wet, being cold, enduring any uncertainty about their schedule or taking any risk of any kind.

'They want the experience Dad had in his village but will only book on a packaged tour. Life ain't a package.'

This got Jodie going. Out of the blue, she announced she wanted to have a child. She was looking for a father. Not so much a father, as a donor. 'I beg your pardon.'

'A sperm donor.'

There's a difference between a donor and a father. She knew there was a difference. She'd rather have found a father for her child but would now settle for a donor. But rather than go to a sperm bank, she'd prefer someone she met by chance somewhere, perhaps somewhere exotic. She wanted more than one child. She wanted them not to make the mistakes she had made and to live long after she had died so that a little piece of her never left the earth.

Thirty-three

I SUSPECT THAT MUM wants to live forever. She is dismissive of any evidence that this may not necessarily happen. On our way to visit Trixie in the House of Lords, Mum lost her footing and fell over in the street. She hung in the air for what felt like eternity before she hit the ground. I could see this happening but could do nothing to help. I wanted to freeze the frame on the second before she landed. But time edged forward. Mum was wearing her best suit and support stockings which had not only cost her a small fortune but had to be searched for all over town. She was far more concerned about any damage to her outfit than about anything done to herself. It was all I could do to get her to sit down after the incident to catch her breath. She didn't want to be late for lunch.

'Are you hurt?'

'Don't be ridiculous.'

'Tell me the truth. Did you get hurt?'

'Of course I didn't get hurt.'

A week or so later, when we were sharing a room in a bed-and-breakfast, I noticed the extent of Mum's bruising. But she wasn't admitting to damage, even then.

Mum is one of those protective mothers who hates it if anybody tries to protect her. She doesn't admit to pain. She tends to crack hardy. One time, after we got back from overseas, she came home from work in the dark, tripped on the driveway and cut her face. She went inside and staunched the blood with a tissue and told nobody. Next day, she got up and drove to the airport to fly to a business appointment up the country. She wasn't going to change her plans, in spite of the fact that the wound throbbed in the pressurised cabin.

'It must have bled like crazy,' I rebuked her later.

'There was some moisture,' she admitted.

Only when she got back to Sydney did Mum stop at the doctor. He put six stitches in her face. None of us knew a thing for another day or two. We got cross at her and insisted that from then on she carry a mobile phone. She got the phone but always leaves it at home.

I wonder why people keep their problems to themselves. I suppose every call for help has the question, 'Do you love me?' lying in the wings. It's a question most of us would prefer to keep off stage because the answer never seems to stick to a script.

~

Our entire culture is an elaborate safety net of stories about love, sex, death and immortality. *Romeo and Juliet* is one of the most popular. The day after we left Florence we found ourselves under the famous balcony in Verona from which Juliet spoke the words, 'wherefore art thou Romeo', probably the least colourful phrase in the whole play but, nonetheless, one of the best known. Verona was already a tourist trap in Dickens' time.

Dickens sat in his hotel room reading *Romeo and Juliet*, remarking sourly, 'Of course, no Englishman had ever read it there before.' This was 150 years before we arrived. The crowds had not gone home. Many of them looked like honeymooners. Love was in the air, but still people managed to jostle impatiently for the best vantage point from which to photograph somebody else's love scene.

There's a statue of Juliet under the balcony. If you rub her breast, you will find true love. Wendy got Hart to rub it for her. Connie said she knew people back in Texas who should come here and rub it and save all the money they were paying to introduction agencies. Ian begged his parents not to rub it. Max said he wasn't interested in finding love until he had found a drink. Jodie rubbed the breast enthusiastically, then got me to do the same, then Mum. Mum approached the task suspiciously.

'I think your mother would look great in really short shorts,' said Jodie.

Suddenly, there was a commotion. A film crew had arrived. They were following the progress of a woman called Angela Williams who was on a tour run by the same company as ours, following a similar itinerary and reaching Verona at the same time, before both buses were to go on to Venice together. The second tour happened to be run by Tony's brother, who looked like Tony right down to the sports jacket.

But Angela was the celebrity. She came from Connecticut, which is not so special. Other people have had to cope with that as well. But Angela was also the oldest passenger in the long history of the company.

When the company was founded after World War I, she was already too old to claim the child's discount. So she waited until both she and her granddaughter qualified for the senior's discount. She was 106 years of age. There was a round of applause when this feat of longevity was announced.

'She doesn't look a day over 100,' said Wendy.

The crew followed Angela as she walked up to the statue of Juliet and rubbed its breast. They weren't happy with the camera angle, so they got her to do it again. The honeymooners all stood aside and shuffled from foot to foot impatiently. It was evident, however, that Angela had not reached 106 by being rushed. She went back to the edge of the square and approached the statue at her leisure. This time she rubbed the other breast, without a hint of the coy rectitude shown by some of the honeymooners. Angela was in pretty good shape. The granddaughter travelling with her, a woman Mum's age, looked a lot more care-worn and stooped than she did.

Angela Williams was suddenly the hero of Mum's life. She had set a new benchmark for Mum and instantly became an idol, a mascot, a totem, a guru, a name with which to motivate and inspire. After this, Mum wouldn't stop talking about Angela. There was no reason, Mum pointed out, why she shouldn't herself be touring Europe when she was 106.

'Just don't expect me to be with you,' I said.

We came across Angela again on the boat that took us from the mainland to Venice. Here she revealed one of the secrets of long life. She gave no quarter to anybody. Rather than apologise for being frail and unable to take the stairs to the lower deck where we were supposed to sit, she simply used her walking stick to intimidate a heavily tattooed deckhand into giving up his seat for her. She won. She sat in the prow like a duchess while Mum made mental notes.

When one of my cousins thinks of Dad, he remembers his last trip to Melbourne. He remembers him getting into the car. Dad wants to visit his sisters, Nona and Patty. Special arrangements are made for his renal dialysis. Fabian is designated as his driver. Dad wants to visit an old friend, a priest, who lives on the outskirts of Melbourne. On the way, they need petrol. Dad wants to know the name of the kid working on the petrol pump. He asks. Dad says he knows someone with the same name in Sydney. He produces a notebook and writes down the kid's name, vowing to find out if the two are related in some way. Dad always carries a Spirax notebook. He always wants to write things down. His handwriting is large and goofy because he has written most things in his life with the pen his father gave him. It has the broadest nib imaginable. He writes down the names of people, the names of streets, the names of places he wants to report to 'the wife'. The kid on the bowser is baffled.

Later, Dad reaches the monastery where the priest lives. It is vast and all but empty. The priest is away. Dad is not expected. He goes to the priest's room, lets himself in and sits at his desk. Another priest finds Dad and is nonplussed. He asks Dad to leave. Dad is annoyed by such discourtesy. He gets back into the car. He tells my cousin that this is what's wrong. This is the whole problem with the church these days. People don't know who you are. My cousin suggests it would help if you introduce yourself. Dad says that's the other problem with the church now. People want to know your business the whole time.

Thirty-four

YOU COULD FILL CANALS with all the ink that has
been used trying to describe Venice.

*. . . what pictures it calls up of lawless, silent adven-
tures in the plashing night*, says Thomas Mann in *Death
in Venice – what visions of death itself, the bier and
solemn rites and last soundless voyage*.

Dickens said that the whole place was like a dream in
which he imagined encountering Shylock or Desde-
mona: *I thought that Shakespeare's spirit was abroad
upon the water somewhere, stealing through the city*.
For Dickens, Venice also stood half way between life and
death, between drowning and survival:

> *Close about the quays and churches, palaces and
> prisons: sucking at their walls, and welling up into
> the secret places of the town: crept the water
> always. Noiseless and watchful: coiled round and
> round it, in its many folds, like an old serpent.*

Such mystical experiences were not on offer in Venice
on July 4. Nearly everyone on the bus was enslaved to

the idea of celebrating American Independence Day. The city was jam-packed. Mum was on top of the world. Her sails were filled with the inspiration of Angela Williams. She asked me if I ever dreamed I'd be sitting in a gondola. She asked me if, when I was studying *Othello* in Year 12, I ever dreamed I would be standing in the Doge's Palace. I gave a curt response to both questions, but did prefer Mum's enthusiasm to Wendy's disdain for the fact that the canals smelt and this was going to bring on a migraine.

'There was nothing in the brochure about odour,' she claimed.

'What did she want,' asked Mum in a stage whisper, 'a sample fragrance sachet?'

It may have been ungracious in a place as old as Venice, with a 900-year-old cathedral, St Mark's, still open for business, but the place I was eager to visit was Harry's Bar. Harry's is one of the most celebrated booze joints in the world. It opened in 1931, which, in Venice, is not even yesterday, but earlier this morning. Its art-deco interior is relatively modern. Since its first days it has regularly shaken cocktails for the likes of Somerset Maugham, Noel Coward, Truman Capote, Orson Welles and Charlie Chaplin. Marcello Mastroianni, star of *La Dolce Vita*, was fond of the place. As was Humphrey Bogart. But it was none of these names which made me interested in Harry's. The customer who fascinated me was Ernest Hemingway.

Hemingway was a writer, of course, but is equally famous for turning the hangover into a cultural accessory. Harry's was one of his favourite watering holes. In his book *Across the River and into the Trees*, Harry's and not the Piazza San Marco is the real hub of Venice. Hemingway must have been well paid, because Harry's is so expensive that you could spend the family fortune on booze and still be safe to drive home. Except that there are no cars in Venice.

I am fascinated by Hemingway because he lived a life that was diametrically the opposite of mine. He liked bullfights and shooting guns. Hemingway was a blokes' bloke to the point of unintentional self-parody. His account of his religious convictions is a case in point. Hemingway rated sex as either 'good bed' or 'bad bed'. There was a period in which he was having 'bad bed' because he couldn't maintain an erection. For a man of Ernest's interests, this was a catastrophe. He tried everything. He even went to see mystics, one of whom used electrodes, another of whom got him to drink live calves' blood. His lover, Pauline, was a devout Catholic. She told him to go to church:

> There was a small church two blocks from us and I went there and said a short prayer. Then I went back to our room. Pauline was in bed, waiting. I undressed and got into bed and we made love like we invented it. We never had any trouble again. That's when I became a Catholic.

Perhaps Hemingway is an *alter ego* of mine; there are some similarities between us. When he was wounded on the Italian front in 1918, he was taken to hospital in Milan, from where he sent his mother a charming letter which included a drawing showing his 227 wounds and a cartoon bubble coming out of his mouth saying 'gimme a drink'. He was nineteen at the time. She must have been delighted by such sensitivity.

Hemingway wrote a number of bar stories, one called 'A clean well-lighted place'. In it, a waiter speaks to himself in the darkness after he has finally put out the light in the small hours of the morning. His words are a mixture of self-pity and John of the Cross, the kind of mixture that makes you wonder where Hemingway is really trying to go:

> *Our nada who art in nada, nada be thy name, thy kingdom nada thy will be nada in nada as it is in nada. Give us this nada our daily nada and nada us our nada as we nada our nadas and nada us not into nada.*

I certainly hope my life ends differently from Hemingway's: he blew his brains out in 1961, a few weeks before I was born. One of the reasons I don't believe in reincarnation is that I won't run the risk of being Hemingway.

Jan Morris, the travel writer, has said that Harry's has not changed in any detail in fifty years. Jan Morris is an expert on change. She began life as a boy and is currently a woman. She is one of the few patrons to have dined at Harry's as a member of both sexes. You have to respect such a comprehensive point of view. She believes that Harry's is one of the great restaurants of the world and doesn't make the mistake of judging a restaurant by the quality of its food alone. Which is just as well, because we didn't eat a mouthful at Harry's.

Harry is a leading exponent of the six-figure menu. Granted, we are talking in lire and anybody who can scrape together a thousand bucks can call themselves a millionaire. We decided to limit ourselves to a single cup of coffee, standing at the bar. This cost twelve bucks. I know where I can buy Hemingway's collected works for not much more. But we enjoyed being there and soaking up the atmosphere. The vinyl cabin bags over our shoulders, our bum-bags and our cheap cameras strapped to our belts like pistols, all added to the glamour. Harry's is tiny. You can see fat tourists squeeze through the narrow saloon doors and ask to be shown the table they will be sitting at before they will confirm a booking for later in the week. It's like choosing a seat when you book a theatre ticket, but, then again, Harry's is a kind of theatre. The whole of Venice feels like that. You can watch a modest-looking plate of pasta dance under your eyes for a moment and remind yourself that there lies sixty bucks. You can easily eat 'not wisely but too well', as Othello once said when Iago added up his bill incorrectly.

The one person we did not expect to see, however, was Angela Williams. Mum squinted in rapt disbelief before confirming her sighting. Angela was sitting in the window seat. She had got rid of the granddaughter who was her chaperone and had flung her jacket nonchalantly over the other chair. She had two bottles of wine open on the table, another in an ice-bucket and a squadron of waiters fussing over her. Angela was an adult before World War I was fought in Europe. And here she was, at the other end of the century, having a $500 lunch in Harry's. You had to hand it to her.

'That's what I'll be doing when I'm 106,' said Mum. 'She's spending the lot before she goes. Every penny. And good luck to her.'

Thirty-five

NAPOLEON SAID THAT the Piazza San Marco was the drawing room of Europe. It has since become the photographing room of Europe. One of our tour members, Danny, kept asking people how many rolls they'd taken.

'I took a roll from the breakfast table,' said Mum. 'We'll need it for Mass.'

'He means rolls of film, Mum.'

'I know that. I was joking.'

Max and Min had thrown caution to the wind and, hang the expense, were walking an unsteady line from one licensed tourist attraction to the next. One hotel had a brass plaque outside saying that this was where Tchaikovsky had composed his most famous ballet. Max peeled off from the group to go inside and ask the tariff on the nutcracker suite. The management had heard this particular gag many times before but Max assured them it was his original. It was only when we got inside St Mark's and began to walk over the undulating floor that Max and Min quietened down. The uneven surface was making them a bit seasick. Countless thousands of visitors have ruffled the mosaics on the floor until they sit like a badly fitting carpet.

The patterns in the floor of St Mark's are made of glass. Venice is famous for glass. I have always considered glass a form of packaging which was elevated to an art form when somebody realised that things look better wrapped in light than anything else. Even windows are a form of packaging when you think about it. They package space and warmth.

The early settlers of the lagoon were refugees. Their heirs are still living here in abundance, trying to sell imitation Gucci to folk who'd rather be fooled by the real thing. The first refugees to Venice were metal workers and it's from the expression for their profession that the ubiquitous word 'ghetto' was born. Either from that or from the word for throwing out your slops. The experts argue about it. It's interesting to think of Venice as the world's first 'ghetto'. In the days after the Berlin Wall came tumbling down, a single day brought 1000 buses of tourists from East Germany alone. One day someone will move heaven and earth to go some place where people worked wonders with cardboard, polystyrene and sticky tape. Angela Williams might even be alive to see it.

It was trade that turned a nation of metal workers into one of glass blowers. They had to move stuff. They haven't lost the knack. After St Mark's, we were shown through a factory where the demonstration on how to sell was as impressive as the demonstration of fine glass making. The master blower looked like a burger flipper going through his paces. We were shown decanters and glasses.

'Are you tempted?' I asked Mum.

'Not on your nelly.'

But her eye fell on a bird which she did like and a salesman adept at reading the least sign of interest quickly sped us into a room full of birds. A glass aviary. It was quiet. The work was beautiful. Mum fell in love with a piece – two birds sitting on a limb. She thought of a hundred and one reasons to buy it and rejected them all. Then finally, reluctantly, she accepted the most persuasive reason of all. She broke one of the habits of a lifetime and bought it for herself.

'Will you take it with you?' asked the salesman.

'No. I think I'll leave it for the family. In my will.'

'Do they live in Venice?'

'Oh. I see what you mean. No, I'll have it sent home by freight.'

The salesman explained in great detail the arrangements for shipping insurance, and the birds were packed with elaborate care before being added to a large pile of similarly anonymous boxes that was building behind the counter. A morning's trade.

'It's also an heirloom,' said Mum, reconsidering her motivation. 'Something I can leave behind.'

~

Jodie, Rae, Mum and I ended up in the coffee lounge of an expensive hotel. We were paying for drinks what you'd pay for the night in a reasonable motel in Australia. Mum felt awkward about being with us.

'I don't want to be a gooseberry.'

'Don't be ridiculous.'

Rae and Mum got talking about Things They Got For

Free. Rae had once checked out of a hotel having inadvertently packed the bath towels. For Mum, an honest oversight of this kind was not theft but just good luck. Mum gave advice on how to pocket important souvenirs such as menus and demonstrated her best technique by blatantly folding the cocktail menu and putting it in her bag. She believes that the best way to avoid suspicion is to act like you own the place.

Meanwhile, Jodie was talking again about wanting to get pregnant. She was talking to me. She said that there was a clinic near her home where they could store sperm so that she could have a second and even third child from the same natural father.

'But I can think of much more fun ways to do things,' she said.

'Like what?'

She laughed, knocked back the rest of her drink and held the empty glass in the face of a passing waiter.

'Same again.'

I may be flattering myself, but I was beginning to think Jodie was dropping hints. I was glad we were in the lobby of a hotel where neither of us could contemplate the price of a room.

'What do you think?'

'Think of what?'

'Do you think I should have a child?'

'On your own?'

'Yes, I suppose.'

I thought for a moment and repeated what Bill had told us about his father returning to his village after forty-three years and how overcome he was to be made to feel like he belonged there, even if for only a day. I then told Jodie the story of the trip Mum and I made to Newcastle and what it meant to Mum to stand on the place her father, John Baxter, had come from. Jodie's kids were likely to miss out on that. They could never go back to the street and the house and the census that proved their deep connection to the river of life. They could never listen out for their grandfather's funny accent and look for the food he spoke about on the other side of the world.

The people of Florence, I said, are desperate to get the poet Dante's remains returned to them. They may have kicked him out of town but he came from the same place they did and that means as much to them as anything he put to paper, even more than the language he did so much to develop. Part of belonging is to come from somewhere.

'But what choice do I have?' she asked.

'Sorry?'

'It's OK for you giving out about this stuff. You make it sound like I'm taking the easy option. Shit. You think it's easy being on your own?'

'No.'

'You think I wouldn't prefer to have all kinds of stories to tell my child about his dad?'

'No.'

'You think I have much choice?'

Thirty-six

FROM VENICE WE trundled on to Assisi, a place that is almost completely identified with two individuals, St Clare and her close friend, St Francis of Assisi. We were well and truly used to the routine of the tour by now. Every evening, your bags went up to your room before you did. Every morning, your bags had to be outside your room before breakfast. The bags came before all else. They had to be carefully marked so that if anything happened to you *en route*, the bags could still get home safely. They were important. After all, they had in them all the stuff you'd bought.

There's nothing much to buy in Assisi. This gives the credit card a bit of respite after it's been working time and a half in Florence and Venice. When the credit card goes quiet, the heart gets a bit of a chance. Most of the people who come to Assisi are in love with it before they get there. This was true for me. In the bus Tony repeated a couple of familiar stories about St Francis of Assisi. Stories about Francis ring like fairy tales, only they are not as prudish as Pinocchio nor as psychologically intrusive as the brothers Grimm. The Francis stories may all have been true, of course, but they are still fables. They have the fabulous ability to set the mind and heart free. That's what underlies Francis' reputation as the first Dr Dolittle, the one who spoke to the birds and animals. His ability to communicate was never caged.

There's the story, for example, about Francis and the ravenous wolf. The folk of a nearby town, Gubbio, were terrified by a wolf which had taken their livestock and killed some of the citizens. It was so ferocious that the normal roles were reversed: the people were trapped. They sent for Francis, who had a few quiet words with 'brother wolf'. According to a medieval biographer, Francis told the wolf that he deserved to be hacked to death. Strangely, these words had a calming effect on the wolf, who gave Francis his paw in a promise to do no further damage. The curious thing, however, is that Francis made the townsfolk promise to feed the wolf for the rest of its life. What the citizens saw as a miracle was in fact a restoration of justice. It's likely that the expanding economy of the town had caused agriculture to encroach on the habitat of the wolf. The wolf had only ever attacked because it was hungry. Francis had set the townsfolk free by calling them back to their responsibilities. The fabulous thing is not that Francis spoke the dialect of the wolf. It is that he understood the alienating language of anger in which the wolf was responding to the degradation of its environment. Francis is honoured as a prophet of peace; I've never known a peace-maker who didn't have the scars to prove it. They all pull anger like a thorn from a lion's paw.

It didn't take long for Francis to become the centre of a cult. He died in 1224 and within two or three generations, his legacy had been baked, trimmed and served to satisfy the hunger of thousands. When his time had come to die, Francis lay on the naked earth and spread his arms in the shape of the cross. A tomb was erected around the site, and then a basilica and then another basilica on top of the first basilica and finally a third basilica. Luckily, basilicas then went out of fashion. If the building craze had continued into the twentieth century, he would have been honoured by having a casino built on top of the basilicas and then a revolving restaurant and finally, an international airport named after him. In a way, just like Mum said, the sheer substance of these memorials to a man who had nothing is hard to come to terms with. Francis was no stranger to irony: irony is any situation where meaning moves on more than one front. But he had a gift for seeing things as they are, a gift that his followers struggled to maintain.

Early biographers had no trouble drawing elaborate parallels between Francis and Jesus. They pointed to the fact that they both had twelve followers and one of them hanged himself. There was also the mysterious stigmata – the wounds which were inflicted on Jesus on the cross were seen in Francis' hands and feet and side. Indeed, the parallels became so close that the person who put together *The Little Flowers of St Francis* had to make some bizarre distinctions. At one point, a fast is described which Francis made during Lent. It begins with the words that Francis was

> *like a second Christ given to the world. Francis went off to a lonely island, without shelter, and took with him two loaves of bread to last for forty days (and nights).*

The medieval writer says that when the boatman came to collect Francis, he had eaten half a loaf, but not because he had been unable to keep the fast. He had eaten as an act of humility so that Christ's forty-day fast could remain pre-eminent. It was an act of one-downsmanship.

~

Most visitors to the Basilica do cast a glance at the crucifix which spoke to Francis at the beginning of his unarmed crusade; a few sit for some moments in front of it. The voice from the crucifix said, 'Go Francis and repair my church which is in ruins.' He obliged. In the shops you can spend as long as you like choosing a replica of the crucifix to take home. There are about twenty types available, including a full-sized one which would pose a challenge to even the most skilful luggage packer.

There's a shop with a range of guns and signs all over the place prohibiting dogs. The storekeeper is apparently unintimidated by the reputation of their local saint as a peacemaker and animal lover.

Another shop, behind the Basilica, has 105 separate types of rosary beads. I counted them. They range from a dollar to about a hundred and fifty dollars. Mum bought a bagful of the cheap ones to give to her colleagues in the pharmacy. She got a few extra as well, I imagined to give to customers who'd tried everything else. We took them back to the Basilica, where a Spanish Franciscan, in the full rig-out, hovered around us menacingly. For some unfathomable reason we had annoyed him. When we went to the holy water font, he moved in on us. He must have decided that we were vandals who would do some of the unpleasant acts in the font which have occasionally happened in the churches I've been appointed to. But Mum dug two kilograms of rosary beads out of her bag and I began ostentatiously to bless them. The friar backed away.

Francis designed the habit that the friar was wearing. 'Designed' is not the right word to describe the famous Franciscan outfit, because design was something Francis tended to discover rather than impose or invent. His father may have been more at home in Venice: he traded in cloth and his travels among Those-Who-Can-Afford-To-Pay took him as far afield as France, from whose monarch he brought back his son's name. The tension between Francis and his father is familiar territory. When they argued publicly over what the boy was doing with his life, Francis stripped off in front of everyone and finally walked away. Before long a peasant gave him a rough old shirt. He found a length of rope which he put around his waist. In this day and age, Francis would have gone down to the local boy scouts' car wash and looked through the bag of wet rags for something to wring out and wear. Maybe Francis would have settled for a T-shirt which said *My father went to France and all I got was this lousy T-shirt.*

Our whole bus had broken out in a bad case of talking T-shirts. Ian had been wearing a shirt for three days which said *Welcome to Philadelphia. Now go home.* He is a master of aversion therapy. We were all watching the shirt change colour from day to day, even from meal to meal.

Apart from Ian and a motorbike rider who had *If you*

can read this, the bitch has fallen off on the back of his costume, one of the reasons that Assisi is so wonderful is because of the simple, earnest chatter of the T-shirts you see around the place. They say *San Miguel Campus Ministry* or *Belfast Buddhists* or *Jesus has never been tried*. Friars walking round in what has become fancy dress do not touch the stones to life nearly as much as a quiet group of young people, wearing their hearts on their T-shirts rather than somebody else's advertising copy.

G.K. Chesterton wrote a great little book about St Francis of Assisi. Practically the only phrase in the whole thing which doesn't bristle with irony is the title. It is called *St Francis of Assisi*. At the end of it, he briefly compares Francis to John Henry Newman. He says that whereas Newman is famous for having written a grammar of assent (in other words, a theory of how to make up your mind), Francis, says Chesterton, *may well be said to have written a grammar of acceptance, a grammar of gratitude*. There's a story that when Francis was going blind, the treatment involved his eyes being cauterised with a red hot poker. Chesterton says:

> *When they took the brand from the furnace, he rose with an urbane gesture and spoke as to an invisible presence: 'Brother Fire, God made you beautiful and strong and useful, I pray thou be courteous to me.'*

His famous canticle about 'Brother Sun and Sister Moon' ends with a warm invocation of Sister Death. Francis did not love nature because it made him feel good. Nature was where he was crucified.

Mum and I managed to separate ourselves from the group and go off in search of the place where Francis was born. Again the venue sounds familiar. It was a stable. Unlike the bare earth on which he died, the stable is one of the few parts of Francis' story which did not become encrusted with art in the century after his death. It is refreshingly simple. A message over the door says *This oratory, once a cattle stall, was the birthplace of Francis, mirror of the world.*

It seems curious to put over somebody's birthplace that they are the mirror of the world. Joseph Brodsky wrote a beguiling book about Venice called *Watermark.* At one point, he stands in front of a hotel mirror and sees his anonymity. The mirror shows him that he is one person among five billion and one visitor among thousands. Look seriously at Francis, and the ego learns the same lesson. Francis is one of the few human beings who saw himself in perspective. (The technique was unfamiliar to those first artists such as Giotto who were captivated by him.) Francis had neither possessions nor achievements to flatter the fragile ego. He was one creature. He knew what the creator had invested in him and felt no need to clothe, make-up, adorn or otherwise pretend that the investment was his own. He said, *I am unable to look at any creature without my whole soul praising the creator.*

This is what Chesterton is getting at when he talks about a grammar of acceptance, a grammar of gratitude. Look at Francis and you see who you really are.

Thirty-seven

MUM WAS TRAVELLING light on the continent. Before leaving England she had trimmed our luggage down, to an extent that other members of the tour marvelled at. Most of what she needed was in her 'dilly bag'. Mum's life has been a succession of 'dilly bags': large shapeless sacks with handles fixed to them so you can carry everything from football boots to ballet shoes. In Assisi she dug into her dilly bag and produced wads of travel literature. I was about to have a go at her for being so fussy about what she brought while still managing to include all this stuff, when she peeled away layers of paper to reveal a dreary brown manila envelope. In the manila envelope was a flabby cardboard folder. In the folder was another photo. It took me a few minutes to recognise the two people in it. It was Mum and her sister as little girls, neither of them yet ten years old. Both have bob cuts and the sort of severe fringes which are obviously the work of a kitchen-table hairdresser.

Francis is famous for having composed a gritty, bittersweet *Canticle of Love*. Mum's picture had a story. The story was also a *Canticle of Love*.

Out of the blue, and with some nervousness, Mum told me that her father had finally become a Catholic because her mother had found out that he'd been having an affair. The condition that Linda put on their reconciliation was that he become a Catholic. Linda wasn't a woman to be taken lightly. I admired her strength but wondered how deep a shotgun conversion could run in anyone's soul. On the other hand, this certainly sounded more realistic than the tale we'd been told up to now about John Baxter becoming a Catholic by listening to Father Freeman's broadcasts between the advertisements for soap powder on Sunday night radio. Father Freeman was admittedly the down-to-earth type who might have appealed to John Baxter. From the radio show he went on to become Cardinal Freeman but never gave up smoking; he used to cut a fine figure outside the church offices in Pitt Street, Sydney, dragging on a smoke along with the secretaries and message boys.

It took many years for the full story of John Baxter's own journey to become clear to me. Mum was a wary guide through the story and let clues drop at awkward intervals. John Baxter was away from home a lot in the merchant navy. His family was always anxious that he'd be on a ship which came to grief. When at home, he often made furniture from timber that he'd brought back with him from far away places, especially from northern New South Wales. One of the few of his pieces which remains is a food cupboard. In the colourful seventies Mum painted it a gaudy orange and my brother kept the chemistry equipment he needed for his hobby in it. It later cost $300 to restore the silky oak to its natural beauty.

It's hard to gather timber on the deck of a merchant ship, so this was a clue: he'd obviously spent quite some time ashore. More time than he should. At one stage he was missing for three or four months, allegedly on business. It turns out that during this time he was having an affair with a woman in Brisbane known to Mum only as Anne.

While he was away, Linda took Mum and her sister, Marie, to a studio portrait session with a photographer called Norton Trevaire. Trevaire had premises in Sydney at 117 King Street, a few doors from Rose's Pharmacy, and this was where the photos were taken. He also had a studio in Brisbane. He was so pleased with how one photo of the two young girls turned out that he put it on display in the window of his Brisbane shop. This was in the early thirties. In the photo, Mum is so little she still has her first teeth. The picture was taken in black and white and later coloured by hand. The colourist's instructions are still pencilled on the back, telling him to give Mum *greeny grey eyes (touch of blue)*, to make her hair slightly darker than her sister's, to make the flowers on their matching dresses mauve.

As Mum tells the story, soon after the photo was put on display in the window of the Brisbane studio, John Baxter happened to be walking past. He was on his own. God knows what frame of mind he was in. Perhaps he was lonely, perhaps he'd just had a fight with Anne, perhaps Anne was pregnant, perhaps he was overcome with self-recrimination. More likely he realised he had two beautiful daughters and fell in love with them all over again.

John phoned home to Linda in Mowbray Road,

Willoughby, and announced he'd be home soon. He gave no indication of what he'd been up to, although I'd be amazed if Linda hadn't guessed. A long-distance phone call, or 'trunk' call as they were evocatively known, was a major event in those days. Besides, Linda was Mum's mother and in similar circumstances Mum would have pieced the whole thing together. Mum never knew anything more about Anne. I feel for Anne. I feel for Linda. John did them both wrong.

Linda said nothing when he got home and John went back to his garden, his carpentry and his cooking. Mum grew up. Stories accumulated. The surface of their life was calm. One day, John found a cat eyeing off one of his birds and swung it round and round over his head before cracking it like a whip into the door of the garage. He went back later to bury it but the cat had recovered and fled.

John Baxter made the matchbox dispenser my sister now uses in her flat. Australia went to war again. Linda announced that the country never had any money for anything during the Depression but the minute a war breaks out, it can find money to kill people. John announced that the war after this one would be between 'the black man and the white man and the black man will win'. This was not a prospect he relished. (Mum stills carries a little of his irrational attitude to other races.) Prince Charles was born and Linda announced he would never sit on the throne. John continued to flout the Sabbath by working in his garden. For years, the same neighbours complained and for years John replied, 'Better the day, better the deed,' never changing in inflection from week to week. He told Mum never to refer to a man as a 'pansy' but didn't say why. He taught Mum his recipe for apple pie. She still uses both his recipe and his pie dish.

Linda set the table stiffly while John cooked. Their daily crockery had been made in Japan and had been a wedding gift. Linda hated it. She thought it was gaudy, cheap and vulgar. Linda expressed displeasure not in duplicate but in triplicate. She thought the gold inlay was particularly cheap, nasty and ugly. Then one day she saw an identical dinner set in the display cabinet at Mark Foy's selling for £450, a fortune in those days. She came home and put the set under lock and key and started setting the table with something inexpensive. She was protecting whatever she had of value. To this day, whenever I say Mass at home, we use one of the plates from Linda's Japanese set.

The issue of John's affair with Anne ticked away in the relationship, waiting for the moment to explode. The fuse took years to reach its charge, but Mum remembers the moment when it did. One day, out of the blue, during an incidental domestic spat, Linda accused John of being unfaithful to her. John thought she must have found out about Anne. More likely she had intuited something from the outset and had sat on her grievance until now. On the other hand, Mum recalls that when John suddenly confessed, Linda was surprised and hurt. You can't blame her.

After the initial explosion, Linda didn't have much idea of what to do with her injury. A cold war frosted over. Linda moved about the house tentatively, rigid with indignity. John spent more time in his garden and workshop. These were his places of order. John was the type of careful craftsman who traced the silhouette of every tool in his workshop onto the white-painted masonite in front of which they were hung. Every time he swung open the door to the workshop, he looked across at that board. He knew at a glance when something was missing. Something had been missing from his marriage for years, but he was not such a skilled craftsman in human relationships.

Some time passed before Linda went down to confession to St Patrick's Church Hill in Sydney and spoke to Father Van Houte.

Confession is a curious practice. Once Dad was told by the priest in confession that he should do something nice for Mum, like take her out for dinner. The evening that resulted was going well until Dad announced over sweets that he was doing this for his penance.

Van Houte had more brains. A French Marist and former missionary, he was a Sydney legend. He spent almost thirty years sitting in the confessional for thirty or more hours a week, offering spiritual and emotional release to thousands of people who came from everywhere to speak to him. A newspaper once quoted him as saying, 'If you come to confession for every little thing, it's like being a spiritual hypochondriac. People don't come to confession because they've lost their temper or said some swear words. They talk about their real problems.' Van Houte told Linda simply to take John along to see another priest whom he recommended. This was Father Donovan, another Marist. After he'd seen Father Donovan, John decided to become a Catholic.

I only met Denis Donovan once. When I was a novice, Mum broke the rules of the Jesuit order by turning up unannounced one afternoon with an old man in tow. He was shy and, had he not been a little stooped, would have stood fairly tall. Mum introduced him. I shook hands formally with the man who had saved her parents' marriage by helping them live with themselves. It was only because she'd been doing Father Donovan a favour, perhaps out of gratitude, that Mum went to the Seamen's Mission on the day she met Dad. In funny ways, I owed him my existence. That day at the novitiate he asked for a cup of tea. That was all he wanted. We talked about the football and the weather and what life was like as a novice. Then we shook hands again and he went home.

It seems improbable to me that John Baxter was blackmailed into becoming a Catholic. I can't imagine either he or Linda thinking that if he converted then they could be reconciled, although it is possible that Linda did think the only chance for his forgiveness was as a Catholic. I think it is much more likely that John became a Catholic for the same reason that people decide to become Christians of any stripe. Not in order to be forgiven, but because they have experienced forgiveness first. There's nothing turns the knees to jelly faster or makes the ego seem so preposterous as being forgiven. When you are forgiven you can see two things at the same time: how ridiculous you are and how loved you are. Forgiveness is the uncomfortable journey from pettiness to smallness.

There were actually two conversions that took place. The other one was Linda's. There's no way John would have been forgiven unless Linda softened, at least for a moment. She was a severe woman at times. We have photos of the two of them, from the middle years of their marriage, which Linda had cut in half. But somehow her view of the world had to bend for a moment to accommodate the fact that John was far from perfect. Later photos of the couple together in their mature years show them relaxed with each other.

Mum skimped and saved and finally bought her first car in which she took them for Sunday outings. Neither of them had ever driven or owned a car. They sat together in the back seat. Late one Saturday afternoon, Linda had a stroke at the bottom of the garden. John carried her inside and she died that night. John did not survive her long. That, alone, speaks volumes about their reconciliation.

Forgiveness doesn't build cathedrals, basilicas and other monuments. You don't forget forgiveness. It's branded on the soul. I wondered what kind of relationship with God needed to put enormous buildings over the place on which St Francis lay naked on the earth and died. I wondered, for that matter, what kind of love needed St Peter's Basilica.

We put Mum's photo on the table between our beds and looked out over the valley as the sun went down over Assisi. Then we found some bread and wine and celebrated a simple Eucharist, a word which means gratitude, an experience we share.

~

Late that night, a group of us sat on the balcony of the hotel enjoying the calm. Mum was asleep. People were showing off the stuff they had acquired in Venice. Jodie and Rae had lashed out and bought the most wonderful collection of masks. We tried them on and swapped them around and did impersonations until we were gasping with hysterics. We had a few drinks.

'I enjoyed our talks in Florence and Venice,' I said to Jodie. I think I was secretly trying to get onto the subject of children again. And then maybe onto the subject of sex. I wasn't too sure where I was heading.

'I wasn't trying to proposition you,' she laughed.

I was caught off guard by her candour.

'I wasn't trying to hit on you,' she repeated.

'What were you trying to do?'

'I was trying to talk.'

'Is that all?'

'I was trying to catch a glimpse of your soul.'

'What do you mean by that?'

'It's not easy to see inside you, Michael. I wanted to see inside you.'

'Did you get a look?'

'I'm not sure that I did.'

'Join the club,' I said, being facetious.

'You always look so lost,' she said.

The moment passed and soon we were laughing again about something entirely different and more tame. We found another bottle and decided that it was too late to worry about sleep. In the early morning, we showered, then packed our bags, went down for breakfast, and got on the bus for Rome, where the group scattered to the four winds. Mum and I stayed an extra day in Rome. I spent most of it sleeping. And looking at the photo of Mum and her older sister which, many years before, had brought home to John Baxter where his heart really lay.

'Did you like the people on the tour?' I asked Mum.

'I never dislike anyone.'

'Yeah. Sure. Did you make any friends, though?'

'I know you did.'

'What do you mean?'

She reached for a familiar phrase.

'I know more than you think I know.'

Dad is getting into the car. We are picking him up from hospital. He has come off dialysis. He has been waiting. The treatment hasn't gone well. It's hot. He is weak. He's in a bad mood. It's my birthday. He's forgotten. He flies off the handle at me because I am rolling down the window of the car. When we get home, I go to my room to cry. Mum finds me. I am ashamed in front of her.

The following year Dad gives me a letter for my birthday. I know he has practised writing it many times with his broad-nibbed fountain pen. Finally he's done his 'clean copy' on special paper. He gives it to me before school. It says 'your birth at 5.30 a.m. on Sunday 29th October, the Feast day of Christ the King, brought me the happiest moment of my life. Praise be to God.' He didn't live for another birthday of mine.

Thirty-eight

WE RETURNED TO England from Italy. Nelson Mandela was in town. So was Holly Hunter. Harrods' sale was on and Holly was opening it. Nelson must have had other things to do.

Trixie and Kevin were celebrating their fortieth wedding anniversary. They had a great location for their party. We had drinks looking out over the Thames from the terrace of the House of Lords. One of Trixie's Labour friends pointed out the old building of the Greater London Council diagonally opposite and reminisced about the days when they used to hang out banners to taunt Maggie Thatcher. You got the impression that he was sorry that things had quietened down a bit. One of Trixie's more conservative friends was interested to hear that I was a Jesuit.

'Have you got your pips up?' he asked.

'I beg your pardon.' I looked into my orange juice, wondering if I had made some kind of *faux pas*.

'Your pips.' He touched my shoulder. 'Have you got your pips up?'

His wife explained that he wanted to know if I was ordained yet.

'Oh, yes, I've got them up.'

'Well then, make sure you keep them up, old boy.'

Jean Trumpington, a fellow peer, spoke on behalf of the guests. Lady Trumpington was the senior party whip, a term that you have to use carefully around the Tories. On the other hand she told the guests that her earliest conversations with Kevin had involved her saying only, 'Ooh, ahh, you're hurting me, Kevin, oooohhhh.' We were relieved when she explained that Kevin had been her dentist.

Trixie spoke about many things that night. She said that when she and Kevin were married in Paris they had to have a civil service the day before the religious one. Kevin went off to the pub after the civil service and left Trixie a note; they didn't consider themselves properly married yet. Trixie also said that she ordered fruit across the channel from Harrods to make her wedding cake, known as the *plum pudding anglaise*. It took Harrods eighteen months to send the bill, and when it arrived it did not seem to imply any particular urgency. Neither delay would be likely these days. Forty years ago was a world away.

~

Jodie and Rae had rung as we were getting dressed for Trixie and Kevin's party.

'I'm in Bath with my aunt,' said Jodie. 'Do you want to visit?'

'We've been there.'

'And done that,' she completed.

I told Jodie that I had decided to get a tattoo.

'That sounds like a great idea,' she enthused.

It wasn't just to displease my mother with one last gurgle of adolescence that I decided to get a tattoo. Looking through the book shop in the crypt of the church of St Martin in the Fields, I'd found a book of Celtic designs which really appealed to me. It was actually a colouring book for kids, but this only made the designs stand out from the page. They were simple, black and white and yet intricate. I thought one of those would make a more lasting souvenir of the trip than the puppets we had bought on the stalls outside for my two nieces. Besides, another friend had recommended a tattooist in Fulham Road.

'Where are you getting it?' asked Rae.

'I've been told about a place that's meant to be pretty good.'

'No. I mean where on your body?'

'Oh. I haven't decided.'

~

There was a tube strike on, so I had plenty of time, sitting in the traffic on top of a number 14 bus to Fulham Road to ponder the best place for a priest to wear a tattoo. In the old days, sailors brought back tattoos from the Pacific Islands as evidence that they had been to the other side of the world. *Tatau* is a Polynesian word. Our bodies are tricky gifts and like it or not they can be read like passports. They tell the story of where we have been and what we've done before we need to open our mouths. Every experience leaves a stamp.

Originally, tattoos were part and parcel of a social context and had ritualistic associations. People wore them like cars wear licence plates: they embedded the individual within a social network which makes London's traffic look relatively simple.

The voyagers of the seventeenth and eighteenth centuries started another trend for tattoos. Far from identifying the wearer as coming from one particular location, these tattoos became evidence of dislocation. They showed the wearers had been somewhere dark and secret. Before long, the technique had also become dislocated and you could have a tattoo done at a place near home, but the wearing of a tattoo was still the mark of dislocation. It was the frontier stamp of the underclass. Fletcher Christian, who made his fame during the mutiny on the *Bounty*, was one of many seamen who had a star tattooed on his chest in imitation of the Order of the Garter. Others took the joke further and had a garter tattooed around their thigh.

Of course, tattoos are far more socially acceptable now than they were even when John Baxter went to sea. Their appeal to me has always been intangible. They make the fact overt that the body talks.

~

The tattoo parlour had a large plate-glass window that faced into the sun. It was hot inside. I noted that the business was extending into the premises next door and took this as a good sign; the artist could not have been infecting too many clients if they kept coming back. As I waited, I browsed among the designs around the room. They ranged in price from £20 to £200, with some special ones marked 'x', meaning the price was available on request. I had brought my colouring book of Celtic designs but couldn't find anything around the walls remotely like them.

I sat and listened to the tattoo gun droning in the next room. There was a two-way window between the waiting room and the studio so that the artist and his client could have their privacy but still keep an eye on what was going on outside. It was not unlike listening to a dentist's drill when you know your turn is next. I started leafing through some of the magazines. Most of them advertised do-it-yourself kits, some quite cheap. One of them had a feature on the creative interplay between tattooing and body piercing and showed a picture of a bloke who had a tiger tattooed around his navel so that when he got his navel pierced it looked like the tongue of the tiger had been pierced as well. Somebody else had done the same thing with a snake.

Eventually, the artist came out, wearing a singlet which showed off his own tattoos. His name was Peter. His client had a surgical pad over his shoulder.

'I'll be with you in a minute,' he said.

He went outside, lifted the pad and took a photo of the shoulder.

'That's a good sign,' said one of the people in the waiting room.

'What do you mean?'

'It means he's pleased with his work. Which means he's in good form. It's a good day to have come.'

'Now, what can I do for you?' Peter asked me.

'I want to discuss some designs.'

I showed him the colouring book and he turned up his nose. He corrected my pronunciation of 'Celtic'. I used a soft 'c'.

'The word is keltic,' he insisted. 'Fucking keltic.'

'What do you think of this?' I asked, showing him one.

'If you ask me, it's not my fucking cup of tea, mate. There's about six fucking hours work in that one, mate.'

I blanch.

'I'll just fix this lady up,' he said.

She came back a few minutes later with a ring in her navel.

'Remember what I said about keeping it clean and for Chrissake don't hang any fucking thing from it.'

I told him to look after the other bloke as well, the one who was glad that Peter took the photo.

'He won't take long,' said Peter. 'He just needs another girl's name on his honour board.'

In a minute, I heard Peter raise his voice over the sound of the drill.

'For fuck's sake, mate, you better spell that one for me. I charge extra for foreign names, remember. They're that much fucking longer, mate. Here, write it down here where I can fucking see it.'

Meanwhile, two young American women arrived in the waiting room. One in a red dress explained that she liked to get a tattoo every holiday. She had three. She showed me one on her shoulder and one on her heel.

Peter and his client came out. Peter had moved into a counselling mode.

'For fuck's sake, if you can't keep a fucking relationship together, you're going to need a new fucking honour board some other fucking place.'

'Have you made up your fucking mind?' he asked me.

'Not yet.'

A bloke arrived to ask about having his eyebrow pierced.

'I can tell you now it's gunna bleed like fuck,' said

Peter. He went through a routine about turning the eyebrow ring in its slot morning and night for ten minutes. The bloke wimped out. I was feeling a bit squeamish myself.

'I haven't had a tattoo,' I explained. 'So I might leave the Celtic cross and start with something simple like the key of life. Just to see what it's like.'

'Well, I can tell you straight that's the worst fucking reason to get a fucking tattoo. Don't do it to see what it's fucking like. They all fucking hurt, mate. They hurt like Christ. It's razor blades passing through your skin, that's what it is. Forget a fucking little thing like that. Come back when you know what you really want.'

Maybe what I wanted was a temporary transfer. From Toys 'R' Us.

Thirty-nine

MUM AND I ended our travels in Paris. This was the final destination of the second of our bus tours, the one that saved us a hundred dollars.

On TV, the Eiffel Tower looks like a scrap yard. Up close, moving gingerly through the fretwork, you could swear you were in a fernery. It combines delicacy and strength even more brilliantly than the Sydney Harbour Bridge.

The Cathedral of Notre Dame does the same. The thing about cavernous Gothic spaces is that they pinpoint you for who you are. Like seeing a photo of yourself taken from a plane. Notre Dame was the last really big church on our travels. It was the one which made me realise how cathedrals are meant to work; they make everybody, from the Pope to the village idiot, able to experience their own smallness as a form of exhilaration. Notre Dame is the home of the hunchback; Victor Hugo says of Quasimodo that *assuredly there was some sort of mysterious pre-existent harmony between that creature and the building.*

It's a pity the hunchback gets trivialised, a bit like Jekyll and Hyde. When we were in London, we noticed the placemats at McDonald's were promoting the new Disney film version of the book, as well as a Hunchback Carnival that was taking place at Disneyland Paris. You could win trips to it. Of course, there's nothing that can't be trivialised by Disneyland, even pleasure. Victor Hugo deserves better than to have become fodder for Disney on the one hand and Broadway musicals on the other. *Notre-Dame de Paris*, the name of the book which let Quasimodo loose in the Western imagination, is a sophisticated meditation on human creativity, especially the forms of architecture and literature. The cathedral shapes the hunchback:

> *you could almost say that he had taken its shape as the snail takes the shape of its shell.*

Hugo says that printing led to the replacement of architecture as *the great book of mankind*. A new acquaintance of Hugo will curse him for the way he lets the story get side-tracked. A friend will see the method in his mad lack of discipline. The story is actually the side-track. As with Tolstoy, Hugo's story is merely the scenic path from one essay to another. The essays are where you stay. One of the stopovers in *Notre-Dame de Paris* is called 'This will kill that'. It is here that Hugo laments the days when architecture, filling both space and time with meaning, did more than the readily available literature which took its place. He was no convert to pulp fiction.

> *In the form of printing, thought is more imperishable than ever; it is volatile, elusive, indestructible.*

It blends with the air. In the time of architecture it became a mountain and took forceful possession of an age and a space. Now it becomes a flock of birds, scatters to the four winds and simultaneously occupies every point of air and space.

If Gutenberg was the assassin of architecture, Disney, Fox and their virtual kith have a contract out on Gutenberg.

~

Less than a hundred metres from Notre Dame, on the fringe of the Latin quarter, is an institution which stands on the cusp of a contemporary revolution in much the same way as Hugo's *Notre-Dame* is poised on the cusp of the one at the end of the fifteenth century. You can see the towers of Notre Dame from the apron outside Shakespeare and Company, one of the most famous book shops in the world. It was opened in different premises in 1919 by an American, Sylvia Beach. During the twenties, Shakespeare and Co was the gathering point of expatriates who, like Beach herself, were in flight from one form of unbearable restriction or another in their own countries. These included Ezra Pound, Ford Madox Ford, Dos Passos and the ubiquitous Ernest Hemingway. It's hard to imagine Hemingway browsing quietly in a bookstore, but there are photos to prove he was there. Hemingway's benign late-life book, *A Moveable Feast*, recalls the generosity of Sylvia Beach when he was stony flat broke; he had worked out a route from his flat to Shakespeare and Co which meant that he didn't have to go past any food shops and torture his empty stomach with the smell of fresh food. That route could not have been easy to find in Paris.

Sylvia Beach did a lot more than just sell books. She also lent them. This must have been a questionable policy from a financial point of view for a book seller, the kind of practice which would have led to the forfeiture of her small-business incentive package in today's climate. But it was lending a book, *Riders to the Sea*, which established a friendship between her and James Joyce. Sylvia Beach also saw *Ulysses* into print. One of those rough-looking first editions is worth a bundle now.

But that's not the point. *Ulysses* is the last brilliant rattle of a certain kind of literate culture in exactly the same way that Notre Dame is the last rattle of a certain kind of building culture. It is a book whose main purpose is to show how even the most simple sequence of events eludes even the most complex narratives, in this case a day in the life of one man in one city. Like *Moby Dick*, it's about the fish that got away. *Moby Dick* is an elaborate web built to snare a single creature. It can't. For Joyce, the elusive fish is meaning itself, or at least the end of a single sentence. The only thing is that, like standing in the hollow spaces of Notre Dame and being daunted, the experience of spending a little time in Joyce's tangled empty web is so exhilarating that you accept your lot.

The current Shakespeare and Co is closely related to its forebear. It is run by George Whitman, who claims descent from Walt. Whitman not Disney. George was, I believe, Sylvia Beach's husband. He is certainly old enough to have served the purpose. I tiptoed past him reverentially and found my way upstairs to where the clutter of books for sale merges unceremoniously with the clutter of Sylvia Beach's library. This is the same library from which Hemingway and Joyce were lent stuff. There are a number of camp stretchers around the library, each with greasy-looking pillows and threadbare towels. George makes these bunks available to importunate travellers, mainly young, who come to Paris on their voyage of self-discovery and have trouble with the hotel tariffs. If you spend a night there, George gets a bit of work out of you the following day, shifting a few boxes and the like. The front room upstairs is still a venue for literary salons.

When I came downstairs again, I found that George had gone outside and was talking with Mum. He had noticed that she was sitting on a bollard and he told her that she'd be more comfortable upstairs, where she could read for as long as she liked and pay nothing. Mum was the only person around about for whom the place was not some kind of shrine.

'No, no,' said Mum. 'I'm resting my weary bones and I'm happy here.'

But George is certainly not running a charity. On English language books the price which is printed in pounds on the back of books is multiplied by twelve to reach the price in francs, which is more than a favourable rate of exchange from his point of view. The shop now has the tendency of many such places to refer endlessly to itself. In the middle of the shop is a table covered with the books that pilgrims to Shakespeare and Co are likely to want to buy if only to be able to say that they'd bought their copy of Henry Miller or Gertrude Stein from George Whitman. There is a pile of paperback copies of *Ulysses* which have on their cover the famous photo of Joyce taken in the shop itself. Each book that is sold is carefully stamped by George as evidence of its provenance.

The table in the centre of the shop has a cat pawing its way into a comfortable position. I wonder how many tourists have come all the way here to buy a copy of *Ulysses* at the cellar door. A studious young American wants to buy one of the Henry Millers but George tells her to put it back because if she is unfamiliar with Miller the book she should start with is not currently in stock. A backpacker flashes a thriller under his nose. George takes a few coins out of his pocket and asks the backpacker to leave the book in the specials box outside as he leaves. He doesn't check whether the backpacker walks off with it or not. Somebody else approaches him with a cookery book and says, 'Isn't this beautiful.' George turns over a few pages.

'Yes it is,' he agrees. 'I'll think I'll buy it. How much do you want?'

'No, no,' says the lady. 'It's yours already. I want to buy it from you.'

At the door of Shakespeare and Co, there is a painted sign which warns that *all characters are fictitious in what Henry Miller calls a wonderland of books.* That's not a bad caption for the place. Like the first generations of readers who returned to Notre Dame, cyber travellers visiting Shakespeare and Co in person may have trouble delineating where the past and present, fantasy and reality, begin and end.

Forty

DAD LIVED FOR SIX YEARS after he was first diagnosed with renal failure. Nobody dreamed that he would do so well. In that time, we got to know Sydney Hospital like the back of our hands. There was an old lift with a driver which used to take you up to Ward 17, the renal ward. The carriage of the lift was an iron cage which enabled you to see the counter weight moving up and down in the shaft outside. The drivers always asked after Dad; he spent time riding the lifts and talking to them during his better days when he was bored. You could take a fire escape from Ward 17 to go and stand on top of the building and look out over the domain and freeway. On winter evenings, after school, I would stand there mesmerised by the swarms of headlights, dreaming I could fly away. Downstairs was an ancient cafe staffed by volunteers. They sold a pie and mash, with gravy, for $1.10. It came on crockery which was so old and thick that it powdered when it broke. In the school holidays, my brother, sister and I lived on this kind of food. The cafe was so cheap that I started to eat a second, even a third, lunch. More time eating meant less time upstairs with Dad.

These were hard years for Mum. Because of her family commitments, she was only in a position to apply for casual jobs and these had a habit of disappearing the minute the person who ran a particular pharmacy found he or she had a distant relative or a friend of a friend who needed work.

Dad spent a lot of time in hospital. We had no such thing as a regular family dinner table. Every day, I filled myself with chips on the way home from school. They worked like a sedative. Mum never sat with us to eat; she was always on the run and ate as she stood over the sink or the washing machine.

'I eat when I worry,' she said.

She still says that.

Mum often came home from work after dark and immediately had to get a meal ready to take to Dad in hospital because he couldn't stomach the regular rations. Mum had a special basket for smuggling hot food into the ward, a practice which was discouraged for patients like Dad who were on strictly controlled diets. The practice could also have been discouraged for the sake of the sanity of the patients' families.

Mum used plastic plates which Dad had brought back from the famous George's department store in Melbourne when he had taken himself off there for a solo holiday in the early days of their marriage. He had wanted to bring back some *haute couture* but, improbably for a newlywed, he hadn't noticed Mum's size. He thought, without realising everyone shared his appetite, that when it comes to crockery, one size fits all. Once the George's plates reached a ruinous condition, Mum started using the plastic tableware she had won by saving hundreds of tokens from packets of Lan Choo Tea. Some days Mum brought the meal home again because Dad hadn't felt like eating. But she went back with another meal the following day. Dad didn't ask for this as a favour. He expected it.

Sometimes I asked Mum why she stuck with Dad. I didn't understand. She loved him. I told her once that she was stupid for what she put up with. That she should leave him. She was visibly hurt. I was in Year 8.

'I know more than you think I know,' she replied.

This was one of Mum's favourite phrases. I later discovered that the words had a distinguished pedigree. It was an adulterated version of the opening of the book that Mum trusted least in the world after *The Sayings of Chairman Mao*. Dr Benjamin Spock's *The Common Sense Book of Baby and Child Care* was the Bible of the baby-boom generation. It was published in 1946 and challenged many of the ideas that had been taken for granted, not just at Crown Street Women's Hospital but all over the Western world. It sold squillions and caused such a seachange that Richard Nixon once accused Spock of corrupting the morals of an entire generation, an accusation which could never, of course, be levelled at Nixon himself. Mum's dog-eared copy lurked guiltily at the back of the same kitchen cupboard in which she kept her 'rods'. These were the broken wooden broom handles she kept on hand for those rare occasions when she could bring herself to inflict a belting on us. Spock opposed corporal punishment. Mum opposed Spock. That didn't stop his ideas seeping into her world. It certainly didn't stop her knowing more than we thought she did.

Spock's first chapter was entitled famously, 'Trust Yourself'. Mum had no problem with this. As she ground through the difficult years of Dad's illness, I think she became convinced that the one and only person on whom she could rely was herself. Herself and the picture of Our Lady over her side of the bed. She spoke to very few people, if anyone, about personal matters. Occasionally, she would bring a particularly grim diagnosis home from the hospital. Once, when I was in Year 9, she came home and told us that she'd been told Dad wasn't likely to see it through the night. She told Our Lady of Perpetual Succour that this wasn't good enough. She didn't ask for favours. She merely stated what was expected. Mum was the boss and Our Lady knew it. Dad scraped through yet again.

~

Throughout the seventies, treatment for kidney failure developed rapidly. Dad went onto dialysis three days a week. He had given up gambling by now but spent the time he was on the kidney machine in Sydney Hospital combing through the form guide in the afternoon tabloids. Suddenly, he started picking winners with unprecedented accuracy. Perhaps it was the additional research he had time for, perhaps it was that he had a clearer head when no money was involved. But Mum forbade him from putting anything on them. His wallet now lived permanently in her dilly bag, out of the way of temptation. Dad wore the resigned face of an heir who couldn't get at his rightful inheritance but accepted the situation. He spent the days he was not on the machine thinking of long lost friends he could ring on the phone. The calls were often intrusive and Dad's circle of friends, never large, diminished even further.

In the final months of his life, Dad started sending letters to people. He was casting out lines. One letter was to the author of a book which happened to mention Dad's father. Dad told the author that if he stuck to the facts, he'd have a budding literary career. He wrote to a former schoolteacher that he hadn't been in touch with for years, to tell the teacher about an old boys' reunion Dad had been to. Dad said, with almost childish wonder, that he was impressed by the sight of so many of his year's oldboys in dinner suits. He finished by saying,

> We learnt many things at St Aloysius College but, most important of all, we learnt that what really counts is not our life in this world, but our Life Hereafter.

'Life Hereafter' was in capitals.

Little by little, the hospital changed as well. The old lift was replaced by an automatic one. We missed talking to the drivers. The new lift tried to eat your feet if you moved too slow. But we got to know some of the orderlies. We found the friendliest ones, the ones who were always on for a chat, were the ones who knew the least English. We liked that.

After a while, Dad went onto a waiting list for a kidney transplant. He had to spend his life close to the phone in case some poor kid with the same blood type and general physical make-up came off a motorbike. Then there would be a rush for the operating theatre. We lived on a knife edge, waiting.

We also knew that a transplant could be rejected. My brother and I were told that one of us would make the best match and that when we reached the right age, we'd be called upon to supply a kidney for Dad. We said we didn't mind, as long as he promised to look after it.

Dad's beloved '46 Chevy was also waiting for a transplant. It needed a new steering column and Dad seemed more concerned to find spare parts for his truck than for his own body. The family spent weekends scouring wrecking yards to find the right column. It was never easy to find parts for post-war vehicles which had only been distributed in small numbers to begin with and we had a number of disappointments when wreckers gave misleading information over the phone. Their places were generally miles away.

Eventually we hit pay dirt. The wrecker concerned lived in his yard, on the bottom floor of an old double-decker bus, surrounded by the remains of the automotive boom of the fifties and sixties. The stairs in the bus were too much by now for his shaky legs and, when Dad asked, he said he'd forgotten what he had up there anyway. Possibly he was resisting Dad's God-given right to inquire into anyone else's business. Perhaps there were the skeletons of passengers who had passed their last stop.

The wrecker had a prodigious memory for cars and had said, when Mum rang, that he had a '46 Chevy Pickup on the lot somewhere. He was as good as his word. What looked to most people like twenty-five acres of indistinguishable junk was, for him, full of personality. He lived with the ghosts of what he called 'great machines'. He rated the '46 Chevy as a great machine.

This opinion won the way to Dad's heart.

'This is a car graveyard, that's what I call it. People don't pay the respect it deserves.'

Dad removed his hat.

The wrecker went away to remove the precious steering column. He gently wrapped it in an old blue singlet and charged $46, a figure he seemed to snatch out of thin air or perhaps took from the date of the vehicle. He sat himself in the driver's seat of the dead bus and gave Mum the change out of an old conductor's satchel. He offered a cup of tea: he had turned the dashboard into a cooking range. Outside, he had rigged up a screen from two car bonnets and created a bush shower around the external mirror of the bus. That way, he explained, he could use the mirror for shaving.

Every morning, on our way to school, we had to kiss Dad on the cheek. I hated this. He would still be in bed. I hated the feel of the stubble on his cheek. I always put my acne cream on first to create a kind of smell barrier. One day, I accidentally scratched him with the bands on my teeth and drew a little blood. He winced. His eyes began to water. I apologised but was secretly, guiltily, pleased.

Dad's truck rejected the steering column. Dad could no longer get a roadworthy certificate and had little option but to give it to our cousins who lived on a property, hoping they might find use for it as a paddock basher. Three weeks before he died, Dad bought a new car for the second time in his life. The next time I laid eyes on Dad's truck, it was slumped in the corner of a paddock, covered in blackberry like a castle in a fairy tale in which everybody has been asleep for twenty years.

Forty-one

MUM AND I WALKED for miles around Paris. In a
strange place, the dependable feeling of a pavement
pushing back at your feet is reassuring. We found the
Jesuit church in the rue de Sevres. It took some searching out, as a shopping arcade has been tacked onto the
front of it and the only indication of a church inside is a
neon sign in the street. We spent more time in the arcade
than the church; the fathers have managed to lease
premises to a better class of retailers and Mum went
through the range of antique perfumes in the Guerlain
shop until she could identify once again, by smell alone,
precisely the one her mother used to wear.

We walked to the Sorbonne and, in rue de Vallette,
found the College Sainte-Barbe. It was here, in the early
1530s, that Ignatius shared accommodation with
Francis Xavier and Peter Favre. Ignatius doesn't say
much in his *Reminiscences* about those days but he
could not have been the easiest rooming mate. He says
that he was once forced to sleep out for a few days
because he had visited a house infected by the plague.
He also remarks baldly (as he later told his secretary)

that 'at this time he was in contact with Master Pierre
Favre and Master Francis Xavier, whom he later won to
the service of God by means of the Exercises'. *The
Spiritual Exercises* he refers to were guidelines for spiritual conversation which he had developed on the basis
of what he'd been through himself.

Ignatius' penchant for 'spiritual conversation' sounds
delightful until you realise how tenacious he was. He
must have nearly driven them mad. Favre, a shepherd
from a small village, was already set on becoming a
priest and probably gave in more easily to Ignatius'
influence. By the time Favre died in 1546 at the age of
forty, he was more than just 'the second Jesuit': he was
one of those unassuming and reflective types who still
inspire enormous affection among Jesuits.

Xavier, on the other hand, was a Basque nobleman
with big plans. He had what the people of New Jersey
call 'attitude'. Ignatius worked on him like Chinese
water torture. Legend has it that Ignatius used to ask
Xavier how much further ahead he'd be if he got rich
and lost his soul.

'What does it profit a man – '

'Shuudduup.'

'If he gains the whole world – '

'Get outta here.'

'And loses his own soul?'

'Shuudduup and get outta here.'

It was Xavier who ended up getting outta there. In
1540, Ignatius oriented him to the East. Xavier brought
his considerable attitude to the task of Asia. He could
have made a fortune selling Amway. He could have sold
tabloids to the queen or a Versace wardrobe to Francis

of Assisi. In fact, he ended up standing out like a sore thumb in the economic rape and pillage of the East. He had nothing to sell. He bought nothing either.

There didn't appear to be anything at the College Sainte-Barbe to mark a 450-year-old friendship which has had no small impact on my own life. When I asked about Ignatius and Xavier, the receptionist said that they didn't have any students by those names in residence. I tried to clarify my question, saying that they had checked out about 1535, but she replied that they didn't have any Spanish students at all. She could not remember ever having had any.

~

We got on the Metro and visited the church in which Trixie and Kevin had been married forty years before. We walked through the Tuileries and found our way to the Musée d'Orsay, a railway station which is now a platform for great art. We were derailed by the work of Rodin, not least his sculptures of Victor Hugo and Honoré de Balzac, both cast in 1897. Rodin captures in two enormous eye-sockets Balzac's legendary sleeplessness, his caffeine addiction, his desperation, and the sharpness of observation which created the 2000 characters in *La Comédie Humaine*. The eyes are hollow; their brilliance is that they simply refuse to follow you. They are craters in his head, deep as wells and bone dry.

We sat for a few minutes on a bench in front of Van Gogh's *Starry Night*. On our left, somebody was snoring loudly. On our right, one American accent was telling another that her self-image had needed working over and that since she had dropped from a size ten to a size eight she had felt 'four sizes better about myself'. There was, as usual, more hushed reverence in the card shop, where people were looking at stuff they might actually pay for.

It's curious that the Impressionists were hitting their straps in the 1870s, at which time the huge church of Sacré Cœur at Montmartre was being readied for the public. We went out to Montmartre on the Metro, went up the steep incline on the funicular and suddenly wondered what we'd hit. There is something desperate about the style of this particular church; it was created to put a lid on the kind of cultural impulses that were giving rise to various isms, including Impressionism. It sits on the hill like an enormous paperweight, an exact contemporary of Vatican I and the definition of papal infallibility. Maybe I have a neurosis about big churches. The artists tended to occupy more modest rooms and garrets in the narrow streets and laneways in the vicinity.

The church of Sacré Cœur was cool and dark after the intense light and heat outside. In spite of the crowds, it was eerily quiet. Mass was getting under way and a number of us took our seats within a fenced enclosure at the centre of the church. Throughout the service, tourists continued to circle round and round the congregation and the altar, rather like the whole event was dead and we were lying in state. It was comforting to be still.

We had come here because it was at Montmartre, the highest point of Paris, that St Ignatius, Francis Xavier and a small band of others (Peter Favre, Diego Lainez, Alfonso Salmeron, Nicolas de Bobadilla and Simon Rodrigues) got together to form the first group of Jesuits. Ignatius was older than the others; both he and

Francis Xavier were mature-age students. Lainez was aged twenty, Salmeron only seventeen; Bobadilla and Rodrigues had volatile temperaments which were attractive in young men but a first-class headache when they reached middle age in the 1550s.

On August 15, 1534, the seven of them came out of the city, into the countryside – as Montmartre then was – and, during Mass, took vows of poverty, chastity and obedience. I have an old bus ticket somewhere which is dated August 15, 1984. I kept it as a souvenir of the 450th anniversary of that day, the uncertain beginnings of the order, because I remember at the time, as a young Jesuit, thinking that the best way I could honour the occasion was to hop on a bus without any idea where I would end up. Just for the day. The first Jesuits didn't have a clue what they were going to do. They just had hopes. Hope became their trade mark, even to the point of absurdity. They believed that where there was death, there was hope.

Such is my grasp of Jesuit beginnings that I didn't realise that Ignatius and his friends actually took their vows in a small church quite close to Sacré Cœur, the Chapelle des Auxiliatrices which is in rue Yvonne-Le-Tac, just a couple of hundred metres away. I was a little disappointed, when we got back to Australia, to discover that we had been so close. But Sacré Cœur does have a special chapel to honour the vows of the first Jesuits. It was difficult to find. After Mass we circled round and round with the tourists, peering into the gloom beyond banks of votive candles, but couldn't locate it. The lady in the gift shop didn't have a clue.

Eventually we found what we were after. The chapel

had been turned into the office of the appeal for the restoration of Sacré Cœur. You could just make out the reliefs of St Ignatius beyond the temporary signs which demanded money to keep the doors of the place open. I thought how differently the words 'rebuild my church' had been presented to St Francis. At least the signs did say that donations would be accepted in any currency. And a visitors' book had been provided for people to pause in their restless movement through the gloom to record their impressions.

'Excuse me being impolite,' one person had written with a failing texta, 'why don't you look after the poor on your doorstep instead of building a monument.'

After they'd made their vows, the first Jesuits went out for a picnic. Mum and I left Sacré Cœur and had a pizza. I was excited.

'He must have had quite a personality,' I said to Mum.

'Who?'

'Ignatius.'

'Why do you say that?'

'Well, he wore down Xavier. And he got those young guys to throw in their lot with him.'

Mum stirred her coffee.

'He was never a mother.'

~

Back at the hotel, Mum mentioned casually that she wouldn't mind visiting a place in rue de Bac on the other side of the river. So off we went. On foot. It was only when we arrived that it dawned on me how important this visit was to her. When we were little, Mum often pinned a 'miraculous medal' to our clothes. I used to find this desperately embarrassing, especially at school. But none of us ever fell through a plate-glass window, got poisoned by sucking on lead pencils or was abducted by aliens, so I presumed they worked. The medal made me feel a bit silly but it would have been worse if Mum ever carried out her threat of pinning a dummy to my shirt to stop me sucking my thumb. Mind you, if she had carried out that threat, she might have saved a fortune in orthodontistry.

This miraculous medal was the very one that Linda had pinned to John Baxter to keep him safe at sea.

The medal has a picture of Mary, the mother of Jesus, on one side, standing with open hands. On the other side it has pictures of the hearts of Jesus and Mary respectively. These images may sound a bit corny, but when you think about it, they are images of tenderness. Mum's faith happens in that well-protected corner of the heart which no logic can bruise. Her faith in her kids is a bit the same. Her trust in a medal is not superstitious. It's more like carrying around a locket of somebody she feels close to.

Mum's not the only one either. We had to wait a little while for the church to open after lunch. By the time it did, there were crowds waiting to get in. There was very little claptrap for sale in the courtyard: you can buy a hundred miraculous medals from a formidable looking nun there for 17 francs, but very little else. Inside the church is the place where Mary is said to have appeared to a nun, Catherine Laboure, on November 27, 1830. Mary asked her to have a medal made and specified the design of the miraculous medal.

'The persons who wear it with confidence will receive great graces,' said Mary.

I find this kind of cultic devotion alienating. All around this church, though, and its courtyard, are hundreds and hundreds of marble plaques which people have put up with the simple message on it: thanks. Outside, Mum wipes away a tear and thanks me for being with her.

We went back to our room and had a massive Chinese takeaway. It wasn't the most delicate cuisine that Paris had to offer, but it did the job. It took up all the room in us which might otherwise have been left for unruly emotions to occupy.

Forty-two

ON THE SUNDAY DAD DIED, Mum was at my bed-side at half past five in the morning. I had heard the phone ringing and gone back to sleep. The call was from the charge sister.

'Get up. Daddy's dead. Get dressed. We're going into the hospital.'

Then she was gone.

We passed across the Harbour Bridge in silence. There was no driver on the lift to ask after Mr McGirr. A priest turned up with his pyjamas on under an overcoat.

Dad was buried later in the week with one of Mum's miraculous medals. She hadn't given up hoping for a miracle, even after he'd died, but I'm not sure what sort of miracle she had in mind. On the day of the funeral, she said that she would never remarry. The fol-lowing day I was allowed the day off school, and we went out for a milkshake together. We were talking about how things had gone. The funeral had been a big event. The church was packed. People had come from far and wide. The music was great. We had been lifted by the kindness of many friends. We discussed how we were going to write all the thank-yous that needed to be sent.

'Yesterday was enough for me too,' said Mum.

'What do you mean?'

'I don't want a funeral when I go. That was enough for us both. That was both our funerals.'

'Don't talk like that.' I was seventeen.

'No. I'm serious. I don't want a funeral.'

'Why?'

'That was enough yesterday. Enough for both of us. I don't want anybody ever to say a word about me. Not a word. When I'm gone, I want to be gone.'

Someone has died. They call the priest and I go to the hospital. I am getting out of the car. I am looking for coins for the parking meter. Shops are open, traffic is heavy, someone is looking for a bin to put an icecream wrapper in, someone is waiting impatiently for a bus, someone is reading a horoscope, someone is talking on a mobile phone. Life goes on. Every time it's different, but every time it's the same. Upstairs, a body is lying between clean sheets. The body is odourless. Paperwork is being finalised. Half a dozen close friends and relatives are waiting for the priest. At least one, maybe a grandchild, will never have seen a dead body before. They stand awkwardly beside the bed. They are sitting in the departure lounge for a journey no agent can plan. They want something to happen.

Forty-three

IN THE FINAL SCENE of *La Dolce Vita*, the trendy young people are beginning to feel the weight of their own disillusionment. They've partied all night and, early in the morning, find themselves on a beach with nowhere much else to go. They discover a sea creature, a jellyfish large enough for them to regard as a monster. It's shapeless and totally out of place. They wonder where it's come from. They think maybe it's from Australia.

The trip between Australia and Europe makes you feel just as glamorous. The journey is as mundane as catching a bus. From Paris we went to London and from London to Sydney. We slept a lot. We watched movies. We ate all the banal inflight cuisine. We browsed through boring magazines. We didn't have a lot left to say. We felt like jellyfish.

~

At 5.30 a.m. in Sydney airport, the entire population of a 747, including the cabin crew, lined up in front of the two cash registers that were open for liquor sales. For

Australians on the way home, the duty-free bottle shop stands like the priest on the way to the gallows. The last comfort in the face of the future.

'Fancy buying grog at this hour,' said the woman behind me.

Most of the returnees looked more eager; there was no such thing as a bad time for buying up grog. The transactions were slow, as most people wanted to put their purchases on a credit card and were discovering that they had left the card on their breakfast tray when the steward came to clear it away. Either that or it was stored in the hold luggage or a partner had just now taken it to the bathroom to pick the rice out of their teeth, just in case the friends and rellies on the other side of customs suspected them of falling prey to foreign cuisine.

'They should have a queue for cash,' I remarked.

'The queue for cash is in front of the automatic teller,' said the woman behind me, scratching her elbow.

We all settled into sullen impatience. Mum and I avoided eye contact. The line inched along, until one man, three in front of me, realised that he was standing on the threshold of one of the achievements of his life. The duty-free rules, he observed to his wife, had been relaxed to the extent that he was entitled to bring in one bottle of spirits, regardless of size. He was going to buy the two-litre bottle of Johnnie Walker. A bottle that big came in a special cradle to make pouring easier. The whole deal was only $199.

'Where are you going to put it?' asked his wife.

'On the bar.'

'How do you know it will fit?'

'I measured the counter before we left home.'

'What do you mean you measured the counter?'

'Otto has one of these bottles, so I checked it out. It just fits.'

Indeed, as the conversation limped along, it became apparent that the only reason the husband had been enticed on this second honeymoon was so he could join the 'Johnnie Runner' club of which his neighbour, Otto, was a member. He was not to be denied. Luckily for the rest of us, his wife conceded. Unluckily, he was presented with a box which was slightly crumpled at one end. It was odd that a guy who had packed himself in a torn T-shirt should be so worried about this, but there was no way known he was going to be satisfied with 'damaged stock'. An assistant was despatched to get a new one, which evidently had to be fetched from the manufacturer's warehouse in Scotland. He made the trip in only twenty minutes. The buyer was satisfied. He smiled beatifically. You could see now that a third honeymoon at some future date was not entirely out of the question.

I met up with them again as we waited to have our passports stamped. By now, several other planes had disgorged their thirsty passengers and every time the queue lurched forward you could hear the merry chink of glassware in the hand luggage.

'Why did you have to make such a fuss? It was only the box it was packed in.'

'The box is important.'

'What for?'

'In case we ever have to move house.'

'When's that going to happen?'

'You never know.'

'I do know. If anybody does any moving, you'll be doing it on your own.'

My last sighting of them was after the box had proved too heavy for him and she refused to help him with it. He was kicking it along the ground towards the passport desk. By then, the box was in a ruinous condition.

Sometimes, when I think of Dad, I think of his body. He dies on Sunday morning. Mum and I go to the hospital. Dad is in a different bed than he was on Friday. Mum asks permission to see him. Then she asks permission for me to see him. We are allowed. Given permission. The nurses have combed his hair. They have buttoned his pyjamas correctly. It looks wrong. He always has the buttons in the wrong holes. You can't see his singlet now. That's wrong too. Dad's pyjamas always fall around him so you can see his singlet.

~

Years later, I am living in a big community of Jesuits in Melbourne. A number of the Jesuits are old. Noel is old. His father fought in the American Civil War. Once a champion sprinter, Noel has had a lifelong reputation for eccentricity. He once went to see a doctor because he had a sore on his leg. The doctor asked how close he sat to his heater. Noel had been burning himself but was too absorbed in his books to notice. At dinner one night, we tease him about his eccentricities. He laughs. He closes his eyes, rocks backwards and forwards in his chair and laughs.

Early next morning, someone looks in on him.

Noel has died in the night. The news moves gently through the community. Before long, we are gathering in his room. The room is full of books and papers. It is cluttered with the empty cereal boxes, cigarette cartons, plastic containers which Noel has salvaged over the years to try and keep his fertile mind in some kind of order. They are full of index cards, photocopies, long lost memos and reminders to himself. It's the same as Cardinal Newman's room. It feels like nothing has ever been thrown out. The room is divided down the middle by an accumulating wall of newspapers, magazines, maps, old diaries, scrap paper and computer printouts. Each item has been added like a twig to a nest.

Noel is lying on a bed that the Jesuits bought from army disposals many years before. It was used by Australian troops in World War I. I saw a bed like it in the war memorial. Two or three others are sitting on the bed with his body. Others are arriving, squeezing in around Noel's possessions, his precious cargo. For a long time, nobody speaks. We are thinking. We are praying. Some of us hold his hands. Nobody needs to comb Noel's hair or tidy up his appearance. Nobody is rushing to appointments. Eventually, there's a pot of tea. After a long, long time someone will think to call the doctor. But there's no rush. No embarrassment. We don't need a doctor to put a name on death. It is part of life. These men are at home. Far more at home, perhaps, with death than with its famous cousin, sex. But this side of the family is the one that is spoken little of. The more reclusive. The harder to befriend.

It is September. In three months, I will become a priest. I am anxious about that, anxious about committing to a Church which seems, at least officially, slow to celebrate an experience of God unless it is packaged in familiar language. Many people's difficulties with religion stem not from the fact that they can't believe but from the fact that they are not believed. But theology, the work of putting words on God, can't be reduced to writing books and making laws. Noel's room is full of paper. We are sitting on piles of it.

Noel's room is also full of signs of love: a cross, rosary beads, a picture of Our Lady of Perpetual Succour. Above all, there are quietly demonstrative men at home with the body of someone they have quietly loved. Sitting in Noel's room, for some reason I practise holding my breath. At the end of each period of sixty seconds without breathing, I am thrilled by the inrush of air. I am glad to be alive. I am glad to be here.

~

I have made many journeys on my own. But not all. Mum and I parted in Sydney; I was going back to Melbourne immediately and starting work the following day. Mum also had to get back to the pharmacy. We were in business mode. We divided up the things we'd bought. We made sure the handles on the plastic bags from the duty-free shop were secure. We collected our baggage from the conveyor. I heaved mine onto the floor, fetched a trolley and followed Mum into the arrivals area. She gave me a quick kiss and kept going. The crowds seemed to part for her and close back in front of me. She is gaining on me. She is getting into a taxi. She is gone.